To mrs. abrams,
     Happy   Chanukah-

Baylin.

Adventures in Friendship

Adventures in Friendship

by CLARENCE B. RANDALL

An Atlantic Monthly Press Book

LITTLE, BROWN AND COMPANY · BOSTON · TORONTO

ATLANTIC-LITTLE, BROWN BOOKS
ARE PUBLISHED BY
LITTLE, BROWN AND COMPANY
IN ASSOCIATION WITH
THE ATLANTIC MONTHLY PRESS

Published simultaneously in Canada
by Little, Brown & Company (Canada) Limited

PRINTED IN THE UNITED STATES OF AMERICA

Foreword

THIS IS a book about people. It is a book of portraits, taken from the museum of my memory, the sort of book which a man enjoys writing solely for his own satisfaction even if no one else ever sees it.

In retirement it is reliving the past to which the mind turns most often for enjoyment, and these are vignettes that record various colorful experiences which I have had with people who have interested me, in all walks of life.

They are not character studies, not serious inquiries into attitudes or philosophical tenets, but just side-ward glances at men and women who from time to time have had an impact upon my life.

The book teaches no lessons, and achieves no purposes, but it was fun writing it. My best hope for it is that it may inspire others in their senior years to find the pleasure that this has given me by doing like-wise before it is too late.

Contents

Adventures in Friendship

Charles M. Schwab

I WAS not born soon enough.

I mourn over the fact that I came into the steel industry too late to have known those bold spirits who dominated its destinies at the turn of the century. Today the chief officers of large American corporations come and go and leave hardly a trace, lost in the anonymity of their vast enterprises. Five years after they have retired the young men in their companies hardly know their names, and when they in turn come to the top and then leave, they too will be soon forgotten. But that was not so in 1900. That was the age of the giants. Their names still persist, and still have a touch of magic about them.

I wish, for example, that I might have known Andrew Carnegie. What a miracle worker he was! His capacity for hard work was incredible, and whatever he touched was transformed by the high voltage which he brought to it. This power flowed from an inner sense of dedication. He had a concept of social responsibility which was greatly in advance of his time, and few individuals in all history have done more for mankind just by their own effort and foresight than he.

Public spirited by his own standards, he was often ruthless by ours. What a beating he gave Mr. Frick! I know, because when my generation came along I picked up for my company some of the pieces that were left over when the Frick empire fell apart, because he could not make his challenge to Carnegie in the Middle West stick.

Nor did I know Judge Gary, that small-town lawyer whose quiet wisdom and clear vision so won the confidence of J. P. Morgan that he went straight to the number-one spot in American industry as chief officer of United States Steel. Devout churchman that he was, he saw no conflict between his code of morals and his management philosophy. He merely embraced autocracy as the rational way of life for industry, and governed his competitors with the same firm complacency that he did his subordinates.

But I did have the great good fortune to know the last of the giants, Mr. Charles M. Schwab. When at the age of thirty-four I was suddenly catapulted into the steel industry, he was our dominant elder statesman, though already coming on into the senior years. It would have been unthinkable for me then to have spoken of him as Charlie Schwab, for the great divide which separated us was vast, but that, of course, was what he was to the American people, who adored him.

[4]

It is not enough to say that he was Chairman of the Board of Bethlehem Steel Company. That was a mere detail. He and Bethlehem were synonymous, of course. But he was far more than that. He was Mr. Steel to the American people.

He was known everywhere. Business leaders sought his opinions eagerly, and no business page in a daily paper was quite complete without a picture of his smiling face, and a quote from him on some current topic.

But his reputation went far beyond all this in one further respect: he was by all odds the nation's most gifted after-dinner speaker. As a raconteur he had no peer, and his latest nifty would spread across the whole country by word of mouth from one club luncheon to the next with incredible speed. In fact, those in the know — and we all claimed to be — were convinced that he had a man secretary whose sole job was to dig up fresh stories for each new banquet at which he spoke. This was quite unnecessary, if true, however, for wisecracks dropped without effort from the lips of Charlie Schwab like petals from a rose, and when he turned on his engaging smile he could charm the birds out of the trees.

He was a fabulous salesman, too, the classic example being that he went to England at the outbreak of the first World War, had lunch with the Queen, hypnotized His Majesty's purchasing agents, and came back with the largest single order for steel ever issued, either before or since.

By nature he was also a born optimist, and this radiant

power of his never failed. At the very bottom of the 1932 depression, when corporate dividends had been cut or passed altogether, and when steel plants had been all but closed down, the press never once caught him off guard. He was always looking into the future with confidence.

Each one of us who fell under his spell has preserved in his memory certain very special vignettes that are forever Charlie Schwab for him, and here are two of mine.

Each year in May the American Iron and Steel Institute holds a series of technical conferences in New York, and then climaxes the proceedings with a banquet, which is a rather grand occasion. The principal address at the dinner is usually made by an important figure from outside the industry. One year, for example, our special guest was General Smuts of South Africa.

With regard to such matters, nothing pleased Charlie Schwab more than to break away from traditional formats, and what he did one year no one but he would have dared to think of, and no one but he could have brought it to pass. Before our astonished eyes he produced as our guest that fabulous personality Queen Marie of Romania. Never before had a lady been present at one of those august occasions, and even on this very special evening none were allowed to be at the tables with the members. To preserve the amenities, however, Mrs. Schwab and a select group of wives were invited to come and sit in the balcony above and across from the speaker's table, where they could look down upon the scene below.

When the coffee had been served, Mr. Schwab rose to begin the festivities. Everything had gone extraordinarily well, he was highly pleased with himself for having thought of this, Her Majesty had captivated everyone within sight of her smile, and our genial host was feeling very expansive. Intoxicated by the general levity about him, and quite without premeditation, I am sure, he suddenly began to tell some very gay stories about adventures which he had had as a bachelor in Paris in earlier years. Involuntarily at one point, he lifted his eyes toward the balcony, where Mrs. Schwab was sitting in the front row in full view of the audience, and since the whole crowd was listening with rapt attention everyone saw this gesture and a titter began to run around the room, which soon broke into universal laughter.

Charlie stopped in the middle of a sentence, held his breath for a moment or two, and exploded into a burst of laughter himself. Then, leaning forward, with a puckish look on his face, he said in a very confidential tone, "Boys, there are times when things can be explained better in public than they can in private."

And now the second one.

There came a May when Mr. Schwab was so far advanced in years that he was no longer chairman of the Institute. Nevertheless, he had been announced as the principal speaker at the morning session. As the meeting opened he was on the platform in the center chair, but Mr. Eugene Grace, his successor at Bethlehem, was at the microphone. He announced that Mr.

Schwab had prepared a paper, but that his health problem made it imprudent for him to stand long on his feet, and went on to say that if the members did not mind he, Mr. Grace, would read it. He had been going for about ten minutes when suddenly Mr. Schwab jumped up from his chair, strode to the reading desk, tore the paper from the hands of Mr. Grace, and said, "Here, give me that! That's the part I wrote." This brought down the house, and the whole gathering roared with mingled laughter and affection.

There has been only one Charlie Schwab, and it is not likely that there will soon be another.

And this may be just as well, for there is a grim side to this picture. Each man must be judged by the standards of his own generation. The contemporaries of Charlie Schwab rated him as a huge success, but he would not be accepted today. He would not measure up as a leader of industry because he was entirely self-centered.

Though cheered to the echo whenever he appeared before an audience, and overwhelmed with envious adulation wherever he went, the truth is that deep down inside he was insensitive to the world about him. It was a field waiting for the furrows which he would plow, and he plowed them most effectively, but always for himself. He lacked a vitalizing sense of social responsibility, either for himself or for big business as a whole. He is not remembered for the libraries he built, the hospitals he endowed, or the scholarships he established. He instituted no pension plans, accepted no posts of public responsibility, and, in general, made no effort to solve the social problems about him, which even then were causing deep concern to thoughtful citizens. He left all that to the next generation.

Money was his god. Not money that could be used to create a heritage for underprivileged Americans, after the manner of Andrew Carnegie, but money that would serve his own purposes, and add to his personal satisfactions. And the sad sequel is that this way of life brought to him its own retribution, for in the end he lost most of his money.

When I was young, I admired this man tremendously, but now I find a tragic note in the thought that one who possessed such extraordinary gifts should have had so little impact upon the total welfare of his country.

2

✧　✧
✧

Benjamin F. Fairless

AMONG MY contemporaries there has been no
man whom I admired more for the high quality
of his business leadership than Ben Fairless.

In the years when he carried the heavy burden that
must always rest upon the shoulders of the president
of the United States Steel Corporation, he displayed a
capacity for industrial statesmanship which has seldom
been equaled in this country. Always resourceful in the
advancement of the interests of his own corporation, and
effective in the administration of its affairs, he never for
a moment forgot that the welfare of the United States
came first.

Yet he was seldom in the public eye. To begin with,
there was nothing unusual or striking about his personal appearance. He was just another well-proportioned
businessman, impeccably dressed in a dark suit. If he
came before a group of strangers in company with other
men, he was not the first one noticed, but when the
meeting was over he was almost invariably the one

who had made the most lasting impression, because of the clarity of his thinking and the courage of his leadership.

His career was like that, too. It was not so much a record of breathtaking decisions eagerly awaited by the press which made an immediate impact upon our economy or the structure of our society, but rather a day-to-day honesty of purpose that found expression in a multiplicity of actions that were right.

On the lighter side, let me suggest one correction for the history of our times. It was not President Kennedy, as is commonly supposed, but Ben Fairless, who introduced the rocking chair as a working tool of administration. He seemed to do his best thinking when gently swaying forward and back, and in those stormy days in 1952, after President Truman seized the steel plants, he took his very special rocker down to Washington and installed it in his suite at the Carlton Hotel. There the industry held its policy conferences, and Ben rocked as he presided, while the rest of us sat stiffly around him on ordinary hotel chairs.

He was at his best when chairing a meeting. Never authoritative, never coercive, but always leading persuasively toward an objective which he saw clearly, he got things done. It was an extraordinary gift. He could promote the most vigorous discussion among strong-willed men who held opposing opinions, and yet arrive at a consensus in the end without once permitting the conference to get out of hand or degenerate into acrimony.

He would have been superb in public life, where

precisely that talent is so often sorely needed, and as I reflect upon his career I am led to wonder what shortcoming in the practice of our democracy causes such men never to offer themselves as candidates for public office. I am altogether certain that never for a moment did such a thought seriously enter the mind of Ben Fairless, and that if it had been suggested to him he would have most pleasantly, but decisively, turned it down. Yet we need such men urgently in the public service. It would not have been a money question, for he was the least money-conscious man imaginable when it came to himself, and what it is that creates the roadblock which keeps men like Ben from becoming candidates for a governorship, for the United States Senate, or even for the presidency is a mystery. I write this feelingly, for I was once myself urged to run for the United States Senate, and turned it down.

Ben also possessed to an extraordinary degree that basic quality which all great leaders must have, whether in public or private life — complete integrity at all times of both mind and purpose. He was incapable of taking a position on any question which did not square absolutely with his personal convictions.

This is how I know.

When I had advanced to the top spot in my own company, it became my responsibility to go to New York and attend the meetings of the Board of the American Iron and Steel Institute. Ben Fairless was then Chairman of that Board, and presided at its sessions. Most of the then members were in the age bracket just above mine. I had met many of them, but did not know them well. As a matter of fact, I did not know Ben either at that time, for it was not until the seizure of the steel industry by President Truman in 1952 that the intimate friendship developed between us which always meant so much to me.

On the day when I attended my first Institute Board meeting, Ben called us to order, then graciously welcomed me, and asked whether I would like to say a few words before he took up the agenda.

On the spur of the moment, I decided to go overboard, for there was something very much in my heart that I wanted to put on the record. I responded as best I could to the amenities, and then sitting up firmly on the edge of my chair I said, "And now there is one thing which I might as well make clear right at the outset, which is this. If prices are ever mentioned in any meeting that I may attend where any of you gentlemen are present, I shall leave the room."

The hush which followed this remark was so thick that it could almost be felt. Finally one of the elder statesmen, with a burst of profanity which left the room blue, said with vitriolic sarcasm, "Aw, come off it!"

Incandescent with anger, I decided that I would leave the room right then and never come back.

But I had reckoned without Ben Fairless. In the same quiet voice in which he always spoke, he said, "Boys, all I can say is that when Clarence goes, I go. Prices will never be discussed in any meeting where I am present."

And they never were.

Then the meeting went right ahead under his chairmanship as though nothing had happened.

In 1952, Ben broke new ground again. The steel strike had been very bitter, and feeling had run high throughout the entire country when President Truman seized all of the plants of the industry. But when at last agreement was arrived at, and the men went back to work, Ben saw that some public gesture was called for to stress the importance on the part of both labor and management of forgetting the past, and working together in genuine harmony. So he invited David McDonald to visit all of the principal plants of United States Steel with him, and that joint tour, which was highly successful, set a new tone for a relationship which badly needed just the sort of conciliation which he brought to it.

As the years passed, our friendship continued to ripen, and when retirement came to us both in the same year — for only a few months separated us in age — we were drawn together in a new affiliation which brought to him an opportunity to greatly widen his horizons, and to me a bit of drama tinged with amusement.

During the summer of 1956, when I was serving on the White House staff, President Eisenhower decided to have the entire subject of economic assistance and mutual security reviewed by a citizens' committee.

I was asked to suggest a man for the chairmanship, and through administrative channels I nominated Ben, but by that time the President was in San Francisco attending the Republican Convention at which he was nominated as the candidate for a second term.

The critical date, according to my diary, was August 23. On that evening Eisenhower was to make his acceptance speech, yet on that very day of days, when every important figure in the party was trying to see him, he and Sherman Adams nevertheless took this matter up and decided it. I had hardly reached my office that morning when Sherman telephoned saying that the President liked the suggestion very much, and instructed me to write Ben to come to Washington immediately after Labor Day to discuss it with him.

Actually, I asked the appointments secretary to extend the invitation, in order to avoid being drawn into discussion of what it was about on the telephone. Ben, of course, accepted, and when the day came I met him at the White House, and took him into the Fish Room for a private talk. There I apologized for still not telling him what this was all about, and explained that in my opinion the President himself should always be the one to present an important subject.

Soon we were called, and were ushered into the President's office. Sherman Adams, Foster Dulles, George Humphrey and several others were already there.

Then most unexpectedly there occurred an awkward contretemps of the sort that can happen easily in a life as complex as that of the Chief Executive. After greeting Ben most cordially, and talking golf scores for a moment, the President picked up a memorandum which had been lying on his desk and began to read from it. I took alarm instantly, for I recognized this as a document I had prepared in which I had discussed such things as budgetary allowances and other matters of procedure. Ben's face showed that he was completely mystified, and I suddenly realized that the President thought that Ben had been asked, had accepted, and that the meeting had been called for the purpose of settling the details.

It is not considered sound protocol to interrupt the President of the United States in the middle of a sentence, but I had no choice. I had to break in and say, "I am sorry, Mr. President, but my friend does not know why he is here."

The President was nonplussed for a moment, but then he broke into a hearty laugh, and said, "Well, Ben, you better accept what I am going to ask you to do, because I have just left my press conference, where I told them about this group and said that my next appointment was with the chairman."

But there was no problem. When the President had finished speaking, and others present had added their comments, no man with Ben's high sense of citizenship could have refused, and he replied, "Mr. President, I am totally inadequate to do this job, but if you ask me to undertake it, I shall of course do so, and I will make it the foremost thing in my life."

Discussions began at once between Ben and the White House staff as to who the other members of the committee should be, and I think that it is an interesting commentary on the times that Ben insisted that Mr. John L. Lewis be asked to serve, and that when Ben himself extended the invitation, Mr. Lewis accepted without a moment's hesitation.

To get under way, Ben called a meeting of the committee and asked various Cabinet officers, heads of agencies, and White House staff members to appear before it and present their viewpoints about the subject of economic assistance.

I was one of those invited. I had some trouble in meeting the schedule, for I was out of the country a good deal at that time, but I managed to make it.

During my testimony, I discussed the convertibility of currencies, which was a very difficult problem at that time, and when the question period came Mr. Lewis said, "Mr. Randall, I don't see why they don't all put a certain amount of money into a common pool, and then issue a new international currency that would be good everywhere."

I was a bit appalled at this comment. I could have gone on far into the night explaining why in my opinion that was an unsound idea, but I wanted to avoid controversy at all cost. So I ducked, I am ashamed to say.

Looking up at the clock, I said, "Mr. Lewis, I have but two minutes left and I am afraid that that would not be enough time to give you the answer that your question merits."

It was easy to see that this annoyed Mr. Lewis, so Ben suavely intervened, and said, "Thank you very much, Mr. Randall, for appearing before us. If we should ask you, would you be willing to come back and appear before us again?"

"Any day," I replied rather jauntily. At this Mr. Lewis, with an impish but nevertheless friendly smile on his face, said, "What day are you in the United States, Mr. Randall?"

That stopped me cold, and concealing my discomfiture under the general laughter, I made my escape. I had the feeling later that this riposte by Mr. Lewis was probably remembered longer by the members of the commission than anything I had said in my testimony.

3

✧ ✧
✧

A Debater at Yale

AS AN undergraduate at Harvard, I wore no white sweater with a large red "H" on my chest, threw no forward passes, pitched no shut-out games, ate at no training tables.

My activity was debating. Never did a freshman yearn more fervently than I to carry his alma mater to victory before the cheering crowds, no matter what the sport, but since I weighed only about a hundred pounds bedside, and there was no athletic competition for midgets, I went out for debating.

We had our moments, though, we debaters. We at least got to visit both Yale and Princeton, though where the expense money came from in those days I have no idea. I could not have traveled farther west from Cambridge than Dedham on my own. Furthermore, we prided ourselves on maintaining the finest of Harvard's old traditions by being impeccably dressed on the platform. We always appeared in white tie and tails, though where I acquired such an outfit in freshman year is now a mystery to me. I suspect that it was from my friend, Max Keezer, the secondhand dealer, but he must have been particularly softhearted for me to have bought it at all. Yet mine fitted me perfectly, though when seen at close range there was a slight greenish cast about it which bore witness to its age.

As intercollegiate competitors, our relations with our adversaries were models of deportment, or perhaps I should say that theirs toward us were. Once my opposite number at Princeton, who was coming to Cambridge to debate on the same evening that I was going there, wrote me in advance, though I had never met him, courteously inviting me to use his room. This helped me greatly, since I could not possibly have afforded to go to the Princeton Inn. Unhappily, our team lost at Princeton, while his was winning at Harvard. This began our friendship, but did not end our competition. Upon graduation from college he came to the Harvard Law School, where we were classmates, and in our senior year he beat me again in public speaking in the finals of the Ames Competition. As the years passed, however, I felt better about being beaten so consistently by this brilliant Princetonian, since he was none other than Chauncey Belknap, who went on to become president of the New York Bar Association.

The moment of drama, however, which I remember most vividly from my participation in debating occurred at New Haven. In my sophomore year I was an alternate on the debating squad and was taken along when the

Varsity went down to Yale. Why there had to be alternates, I have never clearly understood, for I do not recall that any member of the first team was ever carried off the platform injured, as in football.

The alternate did have one managerial function to perform, however. He held the stop watch on the Yale speakers, while his opposite number did the same for Harvard. When I arrived in the hall that evening, I was taken down to the front row and seated beside the Yale alternate. I found him to be a soft-spoken fellow — a little bit older than I, with a warm smile, and yet a sense of deep earnestness about him — whom I liked right off. No one took the trouble to introduce us, so we just sat there by each other, watches in hand, listening to the arguments, and paying strict attention to our jobs.

When the debate was over, however, and the crowd rose to leave the hall, I extended my hand to him in saying goodbye, and said, "My name is Clarence Randall." Then, in that slow soft voice, he replied, "My name is Robert Taft."

I almost fell over. This was the most widely known young man in the United States, and I had been sitting there by him all evening without having the slightest idea who he was.

As the years have passed and I have looked back at that incident, I have often reflected upon how completely typical that was of Bob Taft. There he was, son of the then President of the United States, but possessing such inner humility and awareness of the requirements for good team play that he was content to be an alternate, and hold a stop watch on the speakers, instead of being up there on the platform in the spotlight.

As for the Yale debating coach, it became painfully clear in later years that he was unquestionably right that evening in New Haven in giving my companion the stop watch, and putting him in the front row instead of on the platform. Never in his life did Bob Taft succeed in mastering the art of public speaking. He was born without the golden tongue which we have come to think of as indispensable to the political spell-binder. His words were heavy, and his manner hesitant. Nevertheless, people listened to him. They overlooked these imperfections because they came to sense that he had always done his homework, that he always knew what he was talking about, and that he would never abandon the honesty of his purposes merely to suit the public whim of the moment.

Dr. James Bryant Conant

NO MAN in my generation has been more out-
standing in the diversity of his talents, or the
breadth of his service to our country, than Dr. James
Bryant Conant.

Not being content with merely one distinguished
career, he has had many in succession, taking on one
new challenge after another, and mastering all of them.
First, a brilliant biochemist, then president of Harvard
University, then the United States ambassador to West
Germany, then expert in secondary education, then consultant with respect to teacher training, and then back
again to Berlin at the behest of a Foundation.

How dull in comparison have been the lives of some
of my contemporaries in the business world who have
proven themselves adequate in the roles in which they
were first cast by accident, but who have never had
the thrill of breaking out of their daily routines to
stretch their minds, and search for hidden talents, by
undertaking something altogether different.

As to Jim Conant, I have seen it all from the beginning, and have followed each new step in his astonishing career with affection and admiration.

We met as undergraduates at Harvard, where he was two years behind me. No biochemist I, and no Latin scholar he, so that it was not in the classroom that we came to know one another. Far from it. Our first encounters were in the rather dingy rooms of the old D.U. Club, down the street from the Harvard Union, where Randall the upperclassman helped to initiate Conant the sophomore.

What a motley crew we seniors of 1912 were that year. Not one of us was genuinely solvent, and most of us were on the Harvard dole together. There was Joe Kennedy, father of President Kennedy; Bob Benchley, who became America's favorite humorist; J. Gordon Gilkey, who went on to become one of the great Protestant preachers and religious leaders of our country; Bob Duncan, fund raiser extraordinary for educational institutions; and Oscar Haussermann, top-flight lawyer, civic leader, and humorous poet of Boston.

From time to time D.U. put on plays of sorts. For initiations Gordon Gilkey, who was our class poet, wrote the lyrics and I played the feminine leads, specializing in blondes. Our dramatic high point of the year, however, was the presentation of a pre-Elizabethan drama which no one had ever heard of. Bob Benchley always played the lead, but there was a slight technical difficulty about this, which was that he was not always on the best of terms with the dean scholastically. Once there was a horrible contretemps. Not over a week before we were to open in the "Barn" at Wellesley, "Bench" was put on probation, which meant that he had to withdraw at once from all outside activities. In desperation the coach sent for me and gave me the part, which was that of a cabin boy for a sailing ship, but he said firmly, "You play it straight, Randall! You are no comedian." I have tried to remember that admonition ever since.

My real job, however, was to sell tickets for these shows, and display what embryo management skill I possessed in a rather desperate effort to balance our pre-Elizabethan budget. Here is where Jim Conant came in. He was named as my assistant for the selling of tickets, and ever since I have been ready to proclaim how obvious it is that he profited greatly from my instruction.

Upon graduating from Harvard Law School, I disappeared into the wilderness of the Lake Superior region, and was seen no more for years, but Jim Conant rose like a comet in the academic sky and became president of Harvard. Then, our paths converged once more when out of the murk of the Middle West I began to climb the ladder of the alumni hierarchy. Jim rediscovered me on the banquet circuit, and our friendship began again right where it had left off years before. Then, without any choice on his part, I was suddenly thrust upon him as president of the Harvard Alumni Association.

In that capacity it fell to my lot the following June

to preside at the alumni exercises, which at Harvard are held out of doors on the afternoon of Commencement Day — *Deo volente* — and that brought a diverting bit of drama into our two lives. It is always a gay and happy throng which gathers for that occasion, perched precariously for a brief hour or so on rather ancient folding chairs.

I had made up my mind that as far as my own participation was concerned I would break with tradition, and say some things that had not been said before in those august surroundings. Coming east on the plane, my wife was filled with suspicion that I might yield to temptation and be provocative, and she urged me to stick to the expected formalities, but I gave her the soft answer that turneth away wrath, and kept my own counsel.

I began the proceedings by pointing out that the Alumni Association was well over a hundred years old, and that in the century that had elapsed since John Quincy Adams, first president, had stood where I was standing, he had been followed by an almost unbroken line of diplomats, fiduciary trustees from old New England institutions, literary figures and the like, and that the field of business had been conspicuous by its absence. I then said that if the steel industry would have a chance only once in each one hundred years to speak its piece I must seize the opportunity before me.

So then I pictured a lofty mountaintop to which I proposed to lead the scholar and the businessman in order that they might look down upon the world together. Metaphorically, I pointed out the darkness that was rolling in from every side, and the imminent danger that the light of freedom might be extinguished. Then, turning to the scholar, I urged him to reflect upon the fact that freedom was an integral concept, one not to be divided into separate compartments, and asked him why it was that professors who were so jealous to preserve academic freedom were often the first to threaten freedom of enterprise for the businessman.

When I finished, there came a momentary pause in the program, so I took my seat, which was next to President Conant. His face was a study — midway between smile and frown. He had to say something, so he whispered, "Very good, very good," in a rather formal fashion. "But you didn't like it," I answered. At this he broke nearly into a laugh, and said, "Well, I guess it is all right, so long as it doesn't happen too often."

Then came the unexpected climax. I went back to the speaker's desk and presented to the audience the Honorable Dean Acheson, who was to make the principal address of the day.

His opening gambit was a classic, and those who were present still rib me about it when they see me. Turning toward the president, he said, "President Conant, down at New Haven we have had many bold Robin Hoods in our day, but never one that I recall who raised his standard in the Royal Pavilion itself."

To be president of the Harvard Alumni Association was a deep satisfaction to me, for Harvard meant a great deal in my life, but it also paid Emily and me one very special dividend which we had not anticipated. To see the Harvard-Yale football game is a great thrill at any time, to see it from the fifty-yard line is what all old grads dream about, but to see it from the president's box is joy beyond compare. Yet this is precisely what happened to us the next fall. We had lunch with President Conant and his lovely wife, drove down to Soldiers Field in their car, and sat beside them during the game. Greater bliss hath no Harvard family than that — though the less said about the score in this particular game the better.

The years went further along, and then suddenly one day Dr. Conant announced that he had resigned the presidency of Harvard to accept an appointment as United States ambassador to West Germany. This incredible news completely stunned the academic world throughout the country. They could scarcely believe it. From the pinnacle which he had reached it seemed to them that all paths necessarily led downward. Yet I felt sure that he had done the right thing, and told him so — one of the few who did. He had made a superb contribution to Harvard, but why should he go on indefinitely doing the same things even though from year to year he might do them better? As I see the administrative problems of our great universities, there comes a time when the honeymoon is over. No matter how brilliant the scholar who is at the head of the institution may be, a change may not only be wise for him, but may also prove wholesome for the university in all of the sensitive relationships — faculty, students, alumni, and the general public.

As for the State Department, they could not have made a better choice. He created precisely the image in Germany which was best suited to that difficult period in our postwar relationships. He was Herr Doktor, an ambassador to be revered for his learning in a nation where scholarship is universally respected, and one who could not possibly be suspected of harboring improper objectives of any kind. He had taken advanced academic work in Germany himself in earlier years, and soon he and his wife each had fluent command of the language. Both together and separately they went around the country on speaking trips, thus earning admiration and respect everywhere by the sheer power of their personalities.

In the fall of 1954, when Emily and I stole away for a short breather in Europe, we went to Berlin to visit Jim and Patty, and had a thrilling adventure. Their official duties were such that they had to divide their time between Bonn and Berlin, maintaining homes in each, but luckily for us it so happened that at this time it was their turn at Berlin. We were their first guests in a house which our government had just leased as a residence for our ambassadors. Jim had not even seen it himself before our arrival there, he having flown in from an economic conference in London less than an hour after our arrival from Paris. Protocol is at best a difficult science to master, and it was not until we left the Templehof airdrome that I learned for the first time that an ambassador, when in his automobile, must not only have the American flag flying on the front fender, but must sit in the right rear seat in order that he may raise his hand in salute when the occasion requires it.

Busy as he was, Jim overwhelmed us by saying that he was going to take the whole of the next day off and devote himself to us. We were up early the following morning, ready to leave the house before nine, and neither of us will ever forget what followed.

We first saw something of West Berlin, where we were never out of sight of new construction and where the streets were full of animation, as two and a half million people courageously and hopefully fought their way back toward their normal way of life from the miasma of all but total destruction.

Then we headed for the Eastern Sector, and roamed it at will for hours. This was, of course, long before the wall. Jim said not to worry about taking his time, for it was part of his job to show himself there, flying our flag on his automobile, in witness of the concept that Berlin was a unit.

Things which are commonplace now were new to us then, and as we went along he explained the difference between the Eastern Zone of Germany, which no one entered, and the Eastern Sector of the city, which anyone might. He also cleared up one of my serious misunderstandings by saying that the decision to divide Germany into four zones at the end of the war — British, French, American, and Russian — was not suddenly arrived at by the military commanders in the field, but was one which had been agreed to by all of the four then allies well in advance before any troops landed on the continent at all.

We did not stay in the car in the Eastern Sector, but got out and walked along the streets and into the stores just as though we belonged there, which not many Americans had done at that time. The people knew that we were different, however, and few of them looked us in the eye. Rubble was everywhere, there was seldom an automobile in sight, horses were drawing the carts, and the Germans did not look the same as they had in West Berlin. There was more merchandise on the shelves than we had expected to see, but no one was buying.

The one great exception to the general drabness was Stalin-Allee, which had been created to impress the East Germans with Russia's power. For half a mile magnificent new buildings had been erected that housed really fine stores at street level, and apartments above. But less than a block away the areas were utterly bleak and desolate. Yet there were restaurants where we could have eaten without trouble, and it was said that the opera and the theaters were excellent.

Then we went out to view the memorial built for those Russians who had died while "liberating" Germany. We had never heard of it before, but had to confess that it was breathtaking in its long perspective toward the principal monument, and in the grandeur of its sculpture.

After that we went to see the famous check point on the Autobahn, where the great blockade had begun, and that trip had its moments. For about a mile we were actually in the Russian Zone, as distinguished from the Eastern Sector of Berlin. The geography required it. In so doing we passed a dark patch of woods from which on several occasions passengers on the highway had been killed by trigger-happy sentries, and among the trees we saw dimly the figures of armed soldiers.

We were tired when the day was over, but we felt that we had been on ground where history was being made, and that we had been privileged to be in the company of one who was making it.

When the time came for Dr. Conant to leave the diplomatic service, he returned to the United States and took on a new challenge, one that had long cried out for leadership.

Responding to his own passionate devotion to the cause of higher education, he set out to find a middle course between pursuit of the liberal arts as such in the training of teachers, that their minds might be opened and their horizons widened, and the doctrinaire imposing of prescribed courses as practiced by many professionals in schools of education.

If, as he has said, his objective was to bring to pass "a vigorous national debate on the question of how to educate the teachers of our youth," he could hardly have been more successful. His book on the subject sold fifty thousand copies in the first three months, and wherever professional educators gather it is still certain to be on the agenda for discussion.

What an extraordinary life! Never before that I can recall has one man engaged successively in so many diverse careers, yet not once has he failed to reach the highest level of distinction. To each in turn he has brought the same qualities: absolute selflessness, passionate devotion to the public welfare, and a range of talents that has seldom been equaled in our country.

And when people ask me what it is that I most like about him, I know the answer.

It is his smile.

5

❖ ❖
❖

A Lady from Australia

A GREAT MANY people seem to think that the significant function of the airplane is transportation at high speed.

Not at all. The truth is that the new value which flying has contributed to society is the fact that it compels each passenger to listen to the chatter of his seatmate. Locked in for hours with a person whom you have never seen before and whom you will never see again, you get amazing new insights into ways of life that are totally foreign to your own.

Take pickle making, for example. Here is a commodity which I have long valued at table, but I should have remained forever in ignorance of just how pickles are made had it not been for such a chance encounter.

Then there was the salesman who opened his heart to me about his boss, a beast who would accept any amount of dedicated effort without a word of commendation, let alone increase in pay, but who never missed a chance to condemn some error. The only trouble with that conversation was that I knew his boss.

The airplane adventures which burn most brightly in your memory if you are a man, however, are those where your seatmate is a lady. This seldom happens on a domestic flight. When a lady comes through that front door on the plane — usually in the last breathless moments before takeoff, because she has lingered too long over goodbyes to the relatives — her first thought is to look down the aisle and try to find a vacant seat by another lady. Only if it is the last place vacant will she sit down with a man.

It does happen occasionally, however, on overseas flights where seats are assigned.

For example, there was the very attractive auburn-haired young woman with whom I once flew from Paris to Brussels. I enjoyed her company so much that the flight was altogether too short. She was neither forward in her attitude toward this strange man, nor hesitant. She was just herself, and when I discovered what her job was, I understood, for that quality is the hallmark of the best in her profession. She was a secretary. I liked her particularly because she said nice things about her boss. Though Flemish by birth, she was equally at home in French, for Belgium is a bilingual country. In addition, she had just about as much English as I have French, and we had a good many laughs in trying to communicate, for each of us mingled the two languages in our sentences. She was just returning from two weeks of vacation which she had devoted to a trip to Africa, and she had enjoyed it hugely. She had wanted to come to the United States but had not had money enough. She confided to me that it was common knowledge among her friends that America was too expensive a country for secretaries to visit. Coming in for our landing we flew directly over her house, and as her face lighted up in anticipation, I could see that there would be great excitement in that home that evening as she regaled her family with her adventures.

Nor shall I soon forget the lively conversation which I had with a lady on a tropical March evening in Africa, as we flew from Salisbury in Southern Rhodesia to Brazzaville in the French Congo, crossing the Zambesi River when it was at the flood stage and angry, looking down on Lusaka in Northern Rhodesia just as its lights were beginning to sparkle in the twilight, and coming to our landing alongside the Congo River in the blackness of night with dramatic flashes of lightning not far away on our right. I remember her first of all for her contact lenses, for in my presence she took hers out and cleaned and adjusted them. I had never seen that done before. But I also remember her for her startlingly frank discussion of apartheid. She was a resident of South Africa, and she gave me in straightforward fashion the Afrikaner, Nationalist Party philosophy about relations with the blacks, which I had never heard before.

But there was one adventure of mine with a seat companion from the distaff side which was so bizarre that it outshines all of the others in my memory. This is how it happened.

It was September of 1958, and I was flying back from Europe, having been engaged on government work in our embassies in Lisbon, Paris, and London. The plane was an old Stratocruiser, a piece of equipment which in my opinion was just about the most comfortable that ever took to the air. It gave you a night trip that was long enough so that you could get some rest. Now, in the name of progress, the night flight is so short, and so crammed with food, that you arrive at your destination exhausted, and have to proceed immediately to your hotel and go to bed.

My seatmate was a delightful lady, another who had the gracious gift of falling naturally and easily into conversation with a strange man. Her home was in Sydney, Australia, and she was flying back from Paris by way of the United States.

She had an interesting profession. She was a buyers' buyer in the world of women's fashions. As the representative of all the great stores in Australia which cater to the feminine trade, she comes over about once a year and takes in all of the fashion shows, including those of New York and Los Angeles, as well as Paris, buys single items for copying, and writes reams of reports to guide the buying policies of those who are the clients of her firm of buying consultants.

Since none of this was exactly my métier, I had to be on my guard to transform myself quickly into an eager and responsive listener, without revealing the depths of my ignorance about this unique calling of hers. I remember that I was mightily pleased with myself when, summoning some of my resources, I casually dropped into the conversation the name of St. Laurent, as though it was often on my tongue, and asked her how she felt about the news that he had taken over from Dior. This opened the floodgates, and all during dinner I was enlightened on the history of that earthshaking transaction. It was her unqualified conviction that the new firm would seize world leadership in the field of fashion even more brilliantly than had been done by its predecessor. From this point my education was carried forward until we reached the arresting subject of the change in the hemline, and then on into such an advanced curriculum that in all prudence I had to stifle my comments and rely merely upon "I had not realized that before," and "How fabulous!"

Take, for example, the matter of the ponytail hairdo, which was then the vogue. I had always bowed my head in shame at the thought that this monstrosity was indigenous to America, and that it was we who had laid this curse upon civilized communities everywhere. Not at all. She straightened me out on this, and I learned that in fact it originated in the decadence of Europe, and went on to sweep the world. A young artist was copying a medieval painting of six virgins in a boat, one of whom had her hair done that way. He asked his model to try it. She did, her pals imitated her, and away it went, spreading faster than nuclear fission, and turning out to be just as devastating.

So far, so good. Without more this was enough to give that night crossing of the Atlantic a favored place in my hall of memories, but none of this was the real drama. The startling reality, as I discovered later, was that throughout all this persiflage I was in the midst of a coronary thrombosis, and about four days along, which is the most critical period.

I had been stricken in Lisbon, but with incredible self-assurance had taken no medical advice, had diagnosed it myself as a stomach upset, had gone on to Paris and London, and was then on my way home. Ultimately I arrived in Walter Reed Hospital in Washington, and during the weeks of my convalescence I often wondered what my lady from Australia would have thought had she known the truth about me that night.

6

✧　✧
✧

A Colonialist in the Congo

M Y WIFE and I have an urgent word of caution for those younger than ourselves who have a yen for travel, and it is this: Don't wait. Go the first minute you can. If you put the trip off, it may be too late when next you try. Looking back at our lives from the vantage point of retirement we realize that there is much of the world which we now wish we had seen which we have forever missed because we either could not, or did not, go at the right time. Curtain after curtain has come down in our lifetimes which will not be lifted in the years that still remain to us, and the sad prospect before the modern world is that there probably will be still more to come.

We have always regretted, for example, that we missed China. Emily's mother saw Peking when it was in its glory, including the Forbidden City, went on the Great Wall, saw Shanghai, and did all the then traditional things. Later during the same trip she went on to

Guinea, and then spent time on Bali and in other parts of Indonesia. The story of her adventures when she came back greatly stirred our imaginations. We began to plan at once for the great day when we might do everything she had done, but it never came off. Mao and his cohorts intervened. Now we shall never make it.

Missing Prague and Budapest, however, was strictly our own fault. We had planned to see both of those cities when Emily and I took our first trip to Europe in the summer of 1930, but homesickness got the better of us. We took them off our list while we were in Vienna because we wanted to get back to see the children. We saved them for the next time, but there never was a next time, thanks to the Communists. Now, when the curtain is beginning to lift a bit, we are busy traveling elsewhere.

The same is true of Latvia and Estonia. I had always wanted to visit those hardy little Baltic countries, and had it all figured out. We would do it by automobile, and then drive down across Poland into Germany. Once again, however, we waited too long. Joe Stalin interposed a veto, and we never made the trip.

My luck changed, however, when most unexpectedly President Eisenhower asked me to join his staff, and assigned me to the field of foreign economic policy. I found that I had to get around the world in order to do my job, and it became both my duty and my privilege to see some most unusual places before it was too late. For once I was ahead of history.

The Belgian Congo was one such. I saw Leopoldville before the explosion, when colonialism was the accepted way of life, and the one which seemed destined to go on forever. Yet fate was just around the corner. The time was late March 1958. I had no thought of crisis whatsoever, yet it was incredibly close. By the following January, Belgium had surprised the world by announcing a revolutionary change of policy looking toward independence for her colony, and on May 19, 1960, King Baudouin signed a provisional constitution for the new Republic of the Congo. The period which I had glimpsed was gone forever, and a new chapter in history had been begun.

For the sake of convenience, I based myself at Brazzaville, the capital of the French Congo, which lies just across the broad expanse of the Congo River from Leopoldville, the capital of the Belgian Congo. I have visited Africa many times since, but this was my first swing around that fabulous continent, and I remember that in writing home about my first night in Brazzaville I said, "Africa has to be seen to be believed." Had I not already eliminated from my mind the image of the primitive which so many Americans still hold as the only picture of Africa, it would have been rudely shattered that night. I was housed in a new hotel, built after the manner of our motels, and was kept awake half the night by music and gay voices coming from a fashion show on the terrace, where curvaceous models just flown in from Paris were displaying the latest feminine fashions.

On the morning following my arrival, my first duty
was a call of courtesy upon M. Pierre Messmer, the High
Commissioner-General of French Equatorial Africa,
whom I found to be an extraordinary young man of
about forty-two years of age. This was before the time
when Youlou, the unfrocked priest, took over, and
founded an independent state, but new ideas were already stirring the country. France was worried. She had
long since lost Cochin China, and things looked bad in
Algeria. As a consequence, she was moving rapidly in
her remaining colonies to train Africans in self-government, and prepare for the eventuality of independence
if that had to come. The High Commissioner was perfectly cast for the role, in my opinion. Toward this task
he radiated a high-minded sense of responsibility which
was very impressive. Things were on the move in the
economic sector too, for it was from Messmer that I
learned for the first time that U.S. Steel was about to
enter Gabon to develop a manganese deposit, and that
Bethlehem Steel planned to follow for iron ore.

Yet the primitive was still desperately close at hand,
even as the modern epoch began to take shape, for at
that time within the entire French Congo there was not
a single African who had graduated from a university
in France. In fact, no African had entered high school
in the colony until 1948.

For my trip across the river to visit Leopoldville, His
Excellency very courteously placed at my disposal his
private barge, and that was a colorful experience. The
Congo is a large river, second to the Nile in length

but carrying into the sea a much greater volume of water discharge. Between these two capitals lies the wide Stanley Pool, and at this time there was no regular means of communication and transport to connect them except a small ferryboat, which was invariably crowded and invariably late.

Leopoldville as a city simply amazed me. Gone again was the image of the primitive. The central district constituted a fine modern town of great beauty that would have done credit to Belgium itself, to France, or to the United States had it been set down in our midst. Particularly impressive was the completely air-conditioned new building of the American Consulate General, which was as fine a structure as our government has anywhere. It had just recently been opened by our ambassador to Belgium, who had come down expressly for the purpose.

This was not the whole picture, however, and to get away from this strictly European section of the city I sought out the native market, where I had a fantastic time with my motion-picture camera. It was a vast sea of trading women, clad in bright robes, usually with happy babies on their backs, and never again do I expect to see such a scene. I was captivated, and in all honesty must admit that I thought the Africans here superior to those that I had seen in Kenya and Rhodesia. It had seemed to me that those others were a bit stolid and monosyllabic, but these people of the Congo had lively, sensitive faces, and their conversation, whether with each other or with white people, was gay and responsive. The women wore the most colorful costumes imaginable, and they were extremely style conscious. They did not buy every pattern just because it was vivid, as many a western textile merchant discovered to his sorrow.

But the high spot in my stay, and one of the high spots in my life, in the light of all that has happened since in this strife-torn country, was my conference with M. Léo Pétillon, the Belgian Governor-General.

As I approached his adequate but not at all pretentious residence, before which the Belgian flag was flying, I paused to drink in the unforgettable scene around me. In the foreground was a small but well-kept park, and then immediately beyond lay the river, flowing silently toward the sea, and so broad at this point that the French shore was only dimly visible.

Then I went inside, and for a long and moving period sat across the table from the man upon whose shoulders rested the human responsibility for the development of this vast emerging area. I can close my eyes and see him now, for seldom in my life have I had a conversation which made so vivid an impression upon me — even though I had to do it in French. We had the most intimate man-to-man talk. He may have been wrong, and his country may have been wrong — history will have to decide that — but no one who saw M. Pétillon under the circumstances that I did could doubt his honesty of purpose. He had lived and worked in the Congo for twenty years, and never have I seen a man more passionately devoted to his job than he appeared to be.

He poured out his heart to me in a torrent of emotional French, and seemed greatly relieved that I could sense his thinking in his own language. I had the feeling that he had been waiting for just such a chance to say things that were compellingly on his mind to someone associated with President Eisenhower, and it is a curious twist in contemporary history that the last previous person to whom he had said similar things was Adlai Stevenson, who had made a trip around Africa just ahead of mine.

The Governor-General divided the future development of the colony into three phases, which had to be taken in sequence, in his opinion. The first, he believed, had to be economic. The immediate obligation of Belgium, in his judgment, was to make the area viable, and this involved not only providing jobs for African workers, but giving them training in the necessary manual skills. Next would come what he called social development, by which he meant health, sanitation, and education. Only when these preliminary objectives had been reached in succession could the question of political equality between blacks and whites be approached effectively, in his opinion.

He grew very emotional in expressing to me his ardent philosophy that economic advancement had to come first, and one sentence which he spoke to me so burned itself into my memory that it keeps coming back to haunt me as the destiny of the new Africa begins to unfold. Pausing for emphasis, and pressing his face forward toward mine, he said fervently, "Monsieur, a man

[46]

cannot be free unless he eats." That evening, as I recorded the highlights of this interview in my journal, I wrote this sentence: "Whether he is right, or whether political freedom is a must from the start, is the hard core of the African problem."

No time period was suggested by M. Pétillon which would be required for carrying out the program which he outlined to me, but I had the feeling that he was talking in terms of twenty-five to fifty years. Never for a moment, I am sure, had it crossed his mind as even a remote possibility that within a mere matter of months he would be removed from office, that Belgium would turn swiftly toward complete withdrawal, and that a new nation would be born which would be christened in blood.

As of that time, if my memory serves me correctly, not a single Congolese had yet graduated from a university in Belgium, and the new institution of higher learning for Africans which was being planned under the guidance of Louvain University was just being established. No program had yet been set up for the training of an elite corps in the processes of government, and none for the participation of Congolese in public administration even at the municipal level.

That the French had suddenly begun to move with vigor on all this disturbed the Governor-General deeply. It was his strong conviction that the native population was not yet ready for self-government, and he shook his head with grave apprehension as he made this argument over and over again to me. Once he paused to look out across the broad expanse of the Stanley Pool toward the opposite French shore, then after gloomily repeating his firm conviction on this point, spread his hands and said plaintively, *"Mais, mes voisins,"* meaning, "what can I do if the French insist on their new program?"

Such is my mental picture of this colonialist from the Congo, and I find it a tragic one. Others who knew him better may have seen him differently, but this is how I measured him. Never for a moment did I doubt his personal integrity. To charge him with forming policy solely on the basis of what would best serve the selfish interests of the Belgians would be calumny. He wanted most earnestly to advance the welfare of the Congolese. He may have been mistaken — though that is certainly not yet clear — but he most earnestly believed that he was right, and that is what counts in this world so far as the individual is concerned. No amount of good faith can save a man's reputation if the verdict of history goes against him, but personally I believe that this man tried, and tried hard.

There must have been many such tragic figures during the period of colonialism in Asia and Africa, men who devoted their entire lives with honesty of purpose to the welfare of others, following the truth as they saw it, who nevertheless were rewarded at the close of their careers solely by repudiation and total frustration.

Today when I look at Africa in the light of all that has transpired since that moving experience in Leopoldville, the thought "But will they eat?" still haunts me.

How can a man be really free to pursue his own

ambitions, and to develop the talents with which Providence endowed him at birth, if every waking moment of his life must be devoted to the task of bare subsistence, the mere continuance of his physical being? And even though by some miracle he should lift himself out of that tragic state, how can he still be free if the society about him provides him with no security, no certainty that he can follow where his ideals lead without risking the loss of his life?

When the history of the current torment in Africa is written, the sad verdict may be that it was not the colonies that were freed, but the mother countries.

Responding to the cry of *uhuru,* many of the new nations have won political independence, but as the years pass it may become clear that some of them have also won everlasting poverty and civil chaos.

Take Rwanda and Burundi, two former Belgian colonies, for example. These tiny principalities cannot possibly survive by their own efforts. Their freedom is that of the beggar on the street corner, the right to ask for alms. Meanwhile, they are cutting each other's throats. With Belgian police controls removed, the ancient animosities between the Tutsi and the Hutu groups have flared into warfare, and the slendor public resources available for education and economic development have had to be dissipated by military expenditures.

I pose questions that I cannot answer. It does seem clear, however, that thoughtful Americans should approach these poignant dilemmas with less emotion and with deeper understanding. A way simply must be found in Africa by which whites and blacks may enter into a new partnership, based upon mutual respect and confidence, one in which each will feel comfortable.

7

John Foster Dulles

THE ANCIENT proverb that to be great is to be misunderstood takes on new and disturbing significance when reexamined against the background of our modern democracy.

To those who like myself had periods of service both in industry and in government, the meaning of this phrase was revealed by a disconcerting experience that invariably came to us. While on duty in Washington we came to have deep affection and respect for many men who bore great responsibility, and whose names were widely known, but when we visited our home areas and mingled with our old friends we met nothing but harsh criticism for these same men, whom we believed to be devoted servants to our country. Nor was this a matter of politics. It goes on all the time no matter who is in the White House. Administrations come and administrations go, but this general attitude of all but open ridicule for the leaders of our nation remains endemic.

Men who could not possibly measure up themselves have no hesitancy in condemning those who try to bear those great burdens.

Businessmen are particularly bad offenders in this. They damn all office holders impartially, and implicit in their conduct is the suggestion that they could do the job ever so much better themselves if they were free to undertake it, but that, of course, their present responsibilities are too great to permit that. In fact, the impression which their profanity leaves with you is that almost anyone could do better.

When I reflect on this I am saddened by the thought that I can think of no American who has come to prominence during my lifetime who has been universally recognized as possessing beyond question the quality of greatness, and I am led to wonder whether any of our earlier heroes whose names we now revere so piously, and whose words we quote with such unction, were accepted as great men by their own contemporaries.

This weakness of Americans in downgrading their leaders indiscriminately was the special curse that was laid upon Foster Dulles in his lifetime, and it is one that has persisted since his death. All that his friends can hope for now is that the passage of time may serve to lighten the burden which his memory bears, and bring into sharper focus his many admirable qualities.

I was never a close associate of this distinguished American, yet I felt that I knew him intimately, for during the period when he was Secretary of State I was on the White House staff, and President Eisenhower extended to me the great privilege of attending the meetings of his Cabinet and those of his National Security Council as an observer. There on many occasions of supreme importance I saw Foster Dulles in action, watched the processes of his fine mind, sensed the spiritual quality of all that he said and did, and formed the sincere conviction that he was truly a great man.

He had limitations, as who among us has not?

One was that he had no particular flair for administration. That had not been his métier. He had devoted his entire career to the realm of ideas, and not to the taking of factual decisions, the supervision of others in carrying them out, or the selection and training of personnel. His gift lay in going straight to the heart of an awesome problem in our international relationships, bringing promptly to bear upon it the powerful force of a creative imagination, and coming up with a bold solution. I know many fine administrators who lack that talent, and I doubt whether there are many men who possess both gifts in equal measure.

It is also said that he was not at all times a good team player, and that he was inclined to announce policy without proper consultation. There is merit in the criticism, as I learned from personal experience, when once in Ottawa, without having talked to me, he announced what our policy was on a question which President Eisenhower had assigned to me for study. I took no offense, however. Foreign policy cannot be determined in a town meeting. If it were, nothing would get done, and Foster Dulles was above all else a doer. He was one of the unique personalities of my generation. Often during the period of my government service I asked myself where in the United States a man could be found who would make a better Secretary of State, and I never came up with a satisfactory answer. In fact, I hold the rather startling view that there are more individuals in our country who are qualified to be President than there are who can direct our foreign policy.

Few men have ever come to the State Department as well prepared by personal background for the precise responsibilities which he assumed as Dulles. Statecraft was in his blood, for his grandfather, John Foster, had been in government, and his uncle, Robert Lansing, with whom he was so closely associated, had been Secretary of State for Woodrow Wilson. Even before he finished his education he had become involved in the great issues, and throughout all of his earlier years participation in international affairs had been his passion. His long years in the practice of the law seemed merely to have been intentional stepping stones in his conscious preparation for one day assuming the duties of Secretary of State.

His devotion to the cause of maintaining America's place in the world was utterly selfless. Although he was often involved in controversy, no enemy was ever so mean as to suggest that the policies to which he was committed were influenced in the slightest degree by self-interest or personal considerations of any kind. Men differed as to the soundness of his decisions, but no one ever doubted but that his motives were of the highest.

This great strength of character was based upon deep religious faith. He was as much at home when serving communion in the Presbyterian Church in Washington on the occasion of the President's annual church service for members of the government as he was when taking his seat in the councils of the United Nations. Furthermore, his faith was of the vital, moving sort which often shone through in ordinary conversation. Once in a Cabinet meeting, entirely without preparation, I heard him make one of the most inspiring five-minute talks that I have ever heard anywhere when he expressed his concept both of the opportunities, and of the responsibilities, of the United States in the modern world.

The capacity of his mind was phenomenal. During the long period in which he had been involved in foreign affairs he had touched the most remote quarters of the earth, and his retentive memory was such that he was able on occasion to dredge up out of this past factual data, or explanations as to the conduct of the citizens of other nations, to an extent that made him the despair of the staff which was assigned to brief him. Almost invariably his knowledge was greater than theirs. On the other hand, he was a skilled listener, and possessed an extraordinary facility for receiving and retaining new information on affairs of the moment. In debate he was most resourceful, first because he always knew so much about the subject under discussion, often more than the proponents of the idea themselves, and, secondly, because his fast mind leapt ahead of his adversary. He saw where his opponent would arrive before the sentence was finished, and was ready with an immediate answer.

His critics implemented their hostility by projecting an image of the Secretary as a man who was haughty, aloof, and lacking in warmth of affection for those about him. He did at times create that impression, but it came from his manner, and not from his heart.

He had two unfortunate personal habits which lent credence to this false picture. In a group meeting, when another individual was speaking, Foster did not look him in the eye with an attitude of attentiveness, but doodled incessantly on a pad in front of him. Likewise, when it was his turn to speak, he was apt to fix his eyes on the ceiling instead of looking squarely at those whom he was addressing. This sometimes created an impression of conscious superiority on his part which alienated many people, but it was not the true man at all. Deep down inside he had great humility, and a capacity for warm friendship which was simply overwhelming when released.

Here is how this great human gift touched my own life.

The time was July 1955. In response to a suggestion for the easing of world tensions, first advanced by President Eisenhower, a Summit Conference was arranged in Geneva. Scheduled to be present in addition to the President were Prime Minister Anthony Eden of Great Britain, Premier Edgar Faure of France, Prime Minister Nikolai Bulganin of Russia, and Party Chief Nikita Khrushchev.

Secretary Dulles was to accompany President Eisenhower, and was to fly on a certain afternoon at five o'clock. His life was always complex, but this was the crisis day. Late that morning his secretary called my secretary and asked whether Mr. Randall could come over for lunch. I was simply astounded, and could not possibly imagine what he would want with me at that vital time, but at once I set everything else aside and at the appointed time presented myself at his office.

I was shown in promptly. The Secretary rose immediately, greeted me cordially, and invited me to sit with him on a divan in the corner of his office where a table was spread. He touched a button and lunch came in on a tray — a sandwich for him, and a steak for me.

Still I was baffled, for he gave me no hint yet of what our subject was to be. Instead, he began to talk about Laos, Cambodia, and Viet Nam, which even then were creating difficult problems. I was tremendously interested, but could make little response, for that area lay completely outside my field of responsibility.

Forty-five minutes passed, and then I said, "Mr. Secretary, you have been very kind to me, but this is a difficult day for you, and with your permission I will now go back to my office."

At this his face suddenly beamed with laughter, and with a merry twinkle in his eye he said, "So you want to know why I asked you to come over for lunch! Well, I'll tell you. I just wanted you to hear me say something, and it is this: I like the way you are doing your job down here."

This was so totally unexpected that my voice choked with emotion. I made the best reply that I could, and awkwardly left the room. But as I walked down the corridor I formed in my mind the conviction that has never been shaken in all the years that have since passed, which is that Foster Dulles was a great man.

8

❖ ❖
❖

A Lady from Turkey

NOT ALL of the pictures from the past that come swirling into the mind of a man of senior years as he takes the backward look are happy ones. Inevitably tragedy touches each life at times, and this is the record of one bit of sadness which came to me and which has forever seared my memory. I could not conceivably have imagined that it could happen, and I doubt if many men now living have gone through a similar experience.

In February 1956, I flew out to Turkey on the second of two missions which were entrusted to me by our government during the period of my White House service, accompanied by my good friends and colleagues Forest D. Siefkin of Chicago, and Dr. C. Edward Galbreath of Washington. The White House press release dated January 17, 1956, said that "The governments of the Republic of Turkey and the United States are happy to announce that upon their joint request Mr. Clarence

B. Randall has agreed to proceed to Turkey late this month to discuss economic problems of interest to both countries." I am happy to add that it also said that "Mr. Randall and his associates will serve without compensation."

Turkey was in a financial crisis, and running through the entire dilemma so far as the United States was concerned was the urgent necessity for safeguarding our national security. If we should lose Turkey as an ally, we would risk losing the whole Middle East, and that would be disastrous not only from a military point of view, but as measured in terms of oil and other natural resources. As a consequence, the financial people in our government wanted to be tough, while the Pentagon wanted to be lenient. I was to be the third man in the ring, or, as George Humphrey, Secretary of the Treasury, put it, the "friend of the court." That explains the unusual situation that the request did in fact come to me jointly from the two governments.

I had come to know Prime Minister Adnan Menderes intimately from my earlier mission, which had taken place in 1953, and this time I felt that the cordial reception which he and his Cabinet gave to me and my associates upon our arrival was altogether sincere. We were housed in the official guest house, which was called the Kiosk, and though our time was very limited none of it was wasted by preliminary maneuvering. We went at once into forthright discussion of the issues before us, invariably in a considerate and friendly atmosphere.

As always on such missions, there was more entertaining than we would have wished, but it was all done in excellent taste and with the best of intentions.

The big event of this kind was the dinner arranged in our honor at the Ataturk Farm, which lies just outside of the capital city of Ankara, to which were invited about fifty carefully selected guests. In order that as many as possible of the political leaders upon whose support the Prime Minister would have to rely in carrying out our recommendations might have a chance to look us over, the Prime Minister shrewdly went beyond his Cabinet for his guests. He also included many important members of the Grand National Assembly, which was the name of the Turkish Parliament. Among these was a lady, Madame Nazli Tlabar, a brilliant member of the Assembly (they called it deputy) from Istanbul. She was the only lady present, which bothered her not at all, and she was courteously assigned to me as my dinner partner.

When the time came for us to take our places at the head table, I found that I was seated at the right of the Prime Minister, and that in turn Madame Tlabar was placed at my right. I was indeed fortunate to be between two such stimulating personalities. Each had facile English, and the lady combined a keen mind with a piquant feminine charm which was most unusual. In fact, as the evening went on, I regretted that I had not been born twins, for I wanted to miss no word of what she said, yet I was fascinated by the exceptionally candid things which the Prime Minister was saying to me on the other side about the problems which had been before us all day.

I became so impressed with the nimble mind and sparkling personality of Madame Tlabar that an idea suddenly took shape in my mind, and turning impulsively toward the Prime Minister, I said to him in an aside, "Do you know what you ought to do? You should send this attractive lady on my right to the United States. She could do wonders for you in improving the image of Turkey in our country. I feel strongly that you do not fully appreciate how little Americans know about Turkey, and here is an ambassador who would do you a world of good. Let her make appearances on our television, let her give newspaper interviews, and especially let her get around to our principal cities and appear as a speaker before our women's organizations. You badly need the help she could bring to your problems in the field of American public opinion." He made no reply, but seemed to listen attentively.

On one or two other social occasions which came later, such as a tea one afternoon at our ambassador's residence, I saw the lady briefly again, and always the impression built up in my mind that she was most unusual, but after I returned home I gave the matter no further thought.

Then, suddenly, about a year later, one day when I was in Washington, I heard from her again. The Turkish Embassy telephoned me to say that Madame Tlabar had arrived in the United States and would like to talk with me if that were convenient.

I was delighted and promptly invited her to have dinner with me. She came, and we had a fine evening together. As evidence of the smallness of the world, I remember that she was recognized by an American lady at a nearby table who came over to ours, called her correctly by name, and said that they had met in Istanbul.

Menderes had done exactly what I had suggested. She had been sent over to make public appearances in the United States in the hope that she might thereby improve the understanding of Turkey's problems among Americans. I listened more than I talked, for she was extremely articulate about her country, and had all the zeal of a missionary. But once again, after I had driven her back to the residence of a member of the staff of the Turkish Embassy where she was staying, she passed out of my mind.

Then came the explosion, and my hour of anguish.

In 1960 the Turkey which I had known was blown apart by revolution, and the Menderes government was overthrown by a coup d'etat. The Prime Minister was arrested, imprisoned for a long time on an island in the Bosphorus, and eventually executed. At the same time a large number of his political associates were likewise seized and thrown into jail to await trial for treason.

Among these was Madame Tlabar.

This sudden outburst of terror was very difficult for me to accept, and my heart was filled with both sympathy and anger. I had known personally not only Menderes himself, but a great many of the former public officials who were now imprisoned, including Madame Tlabar, and had thought of them as friends. It was shocking to me to learn that they were now all charged with crime, yet I was at the White House, and my conscience told me that I was not free to express myself as an individual, while I was a member of the government, on a matter that was not within my field of responsibility. Furthermore, I knew that it was not right for me to form judgments and express opinions as to the merits of the controversy without having heard what was to be said on the other side. As for the whole question of the moral basis for overthrowing an existing government, I remembered that my own country was brought into being by a revolution.

I was particularly apprehensive about the fate of Madame Tlabar, for it seemed to me that she was a follower of policy rather than one who created it, but all that I could learn was that she would soon be brought to trial. I had never met her husband, and could think of no one to whom I could write and make a direct inquiry.

Then came the letter. Most unexpectedly there was delivered to me a communication addressed to me at the White House from a Turk, who had known of my acquaintance with this lady deputy from Istanbul. He said that she was in peril for her life, and that she desperately needed my help. He asked me most urgently to intervene in her behalf before the court which had been charged by the new government with investigating the alleged crimes of those who had been detained. He asked me specifically to forward to the court for her defense a statement saying that she had been sent to the United States by the Prime Minister upon my recommendation, and expressing the opinion that the services which she had thus rendered had been beneficial to Turkey. He intimated that in this way and in no other could her life be saved.

Seldom have I been more deeply disturbed than I was when I opened that letter. The fate of another human being, the question of whether she should live or die, had been placed in my hands. Not to reply might mean sending Madame Tlabar to the firing squad. I have great faith in the honesty of the Turkish people, and I was confident that they would believe me if I sent the statement. It might be that I could thus save a human life. My instinct was to act immediately, and do precisely what had been asked, but I was determined not to be guilty of rash conduct, so I restrained that impulse and reflected upon the matter for two or three days.

Then sober thought prevailed and stayed my hand. I knew that I had no standing whatever in Turkey except that which arose from the fact that I had twice been sent there as a representative of President Eisenhower. It was actually his influence which this Turk was seeking to bring to bear upon the problem of a single individual, and I had no right thus to run the risk of creating an international incident between the two governments when the United States had so much at stake in Turkey. What was involved here was the sovereignty of another nation, and I had no right by indirection to place the

United States in the position of purporting to intrude within that sovereignty.

So in sadness I closed this chapter in my life.

With a heavy heart I replied that I could not send on the statement which had been requested, and to this day I do not know what became of my lady from Turkey.

9

✧　✧
✧

Philip Murray

WHEN IN the late thirties the first great labor
storm broke, and a sudden wave of organizing
strikes swept across the country to build membership
for the new mass unions, neither side in the conflict was
ready. Violence and civil disturbance broke out in nearly
all of the large centers of employment, the reasons for
which are now clear. The new union leaders were intoxicated by thirst for power, but were totally unprepared
for assuming the leadership which they were creating,
while stunned management was determined to preserve
the status quo no matter what that might require. It
was a mad, mad period. We now know that had there
been on the two sides enough men of even temper and
broad industrial statesmanship, men possessed of deep
understanding of human relationships, much of this
chaos could have been avoided, but none of us saw
that then.

Certainly the steel industry was not ready, and the

situation in my company must have been typical. A revolution was in process, and armed mobs were hammering at the gates of the steel plant threatening to destroy it, before we had any plan of what to do about it. We knew nothing whatever about unions. No senior executive of the company, and no operating official at the mill had ever faced such a situation before. No one among us had been trained in what is now known as industrial relations, and there would have been no institution at which we might have received such training had we sensed that we needed it.

Nevertheless, ready or not, someone had to be given this responsibility, for decisions had to be made and policies formulated, and I suppose that many corporations did what mine did. It gave it to the only man who happened to have legal training, namely me. But I was no more ready than anyone else. I had never met a union leader, had never seen a strike, and knew no labor law, but there was no time to lose, and I was thrown off the deep end. Overnight, when the mass picketing hit us, the plant management began arming the supervisory force with shotguns that carried rock salt instead of lead in the shells, and I flew down to the state Capitol to ask the Governor to call out the National Guard to preserve order.

The man behind all this frenzy of strikes for the organization of the workers was Phil Murray, creator of the CIO. He was the arch-demon from the management viewpoint, the architect of all this violence. Never once did it cross our minds that perhaps here was a man who thought that our conduct was as irresponsible and reprehensible as we conceived his to be.

In later years Phil Murray and I were destined to know each other intimately, but in this early period I not only had not met him, but had not the slightest desire to do so. At that time, I would no more have considered sitting down voluntarily across the table from him, let alone inviting him to lunch, than I would if he had been Beelzebub. He was complete anathema to me.

But the passing of the years brought its mollifying influence to bear upon my fury. Gradually Phil Murray and I began to move into the same orbit, and the more I saw of him the more my attitude toward him improved, as it did in fact toward the whole union movement. Finally we came to know each other as intimately as two adversaries ever may. Always we were on opposite sides of the bargaining table, always we spoke out in candor, and carried on our contests with vigor, but into this unusual relationship there came a new and surprising element. I not only began to have great respect for this labor leader, but to sense a warmth toward him that was very close to affection, and I have the feeling that he reacted that way about me, too.

When the circumstances were such that Phil was free to relax, and did not feel compelled to take a tough posture in order to impress his followers, he was a man of great personal charm. Those large and lustrous brown eyes were warm and human, and lurking in them was often a subtle twinkle of quiet merriment. His voice was captivating, too. He spoke slowly, in a mood of gentle dignity, articulated clearly, and gave to each word the Scotch burr which was his hallmark. In fact, I can now confess that on various occasions during those stormy times, when perturbed management would be relaxing of an evening, I used to be called upon to do an imitation of Phil Murray testifying at a labor hearing. It began, "Mr. Chairman, and honorable members of this Commission, on behalf of the organization which I am privileged to represent may I say," etc. Those are the words, but no printed page can capture his inimitable manner, or reproduce that burr.

I acquired this special skill for burlesquing the manner and speech of Phil Murray by virtue of the fact that in 1943 I was locked in with him in mortal combat before a labor fact-finding board in Washington for a continuous period of fourteen weeks. By the cosmic accidents which seem to govern these matters, my company was the target that year, with the result that as Inland went so would go the industry. Five cents an hour was the principal obstacle that divided us during all those sessions, and I can still see the impish smile on his face as he would meet us in the corridor during recess and say, "When you gonna quit and give us that lousy nickel?" This was typical. He would be hard-fisted and cold in public, and then not show the slightest personal animosity when he was alone with you in private conversation.

More years passed, and there came the night in New York when before a large audience gathered under the auspices of the National Industrial Conference Board, Phil Murray and I put on a joint debate. He spoke first, and I watched the faces of the listeners with the keenest interest. They had come in a growling mood, expecting to be made very mad, but that was not what happened. Instead they heard a man who was modest in manner, who made a well-reasoned argument, and one who never once raised his voice in anger. They did not agree with what he said, but try as they would they could not dislike the man. When my turn came, I opened by saying, "My friends, you think you have heard the real Phil Murray tonight, and I submit that he has been delightful to listen to, but if you really want to see him in action you must bring about six hundred of his boys here, put them in the back of the hall, and let him talk to them while you listen."

That was the night that Phil promoted me, the earliest time when he used my first name. After the meeting was over, when we were saying goodnight, he came close to me and said, "Clarence, I want you to do something for me. I want you to address the next annual convention of the CIO." I was so astonished that I stumbled in my answer — in part because I knew that since I was only a vice president of my company I should go back and ask the boss. Actually I wanted very much to accept, so I gave him a reply that kept the door open. The question became moot, however, for when the next convention came along I was not asked, and I have always assumed that his staff turned thumbs down on me.

Our major encounter came, however, during the steel

strike of 1952, at the time when President Truman seized the steel industry, and it fell to my lot to be the spokesman for the major producers in challenging the action of the President on a nationwide television appearance. After the court had held that the seizure of the plants was without foundation in law, something had to be done about the strike, and the President called both sides to the White House for further collective bargaining under his watchful eye.

We met for those sessions in the Cabinet Room, with the chief officers of the companies on one side of the conference table, and the union officials on the other. By accident I sat across from Phil Murray, and we glowered at one another hour after hour.

When we came together for the first time after my television appearance, he opened the session by giving me a tongue lashing the like of which I have never received on any other occasion in my whole life, before or since. He was in a towering rage, but when the mood was upon him he did not roar; he merely spoke more words to the minute and held himself absolutely rigid in the intensity of his passion. He cried out, "You are just a plain coward. You hid behind that television screen where nobody could get at you to answer you. You haven't got the guts to stand up and say those same things before the only people who count in this matter — the workers. I dare you to do just that. We will fly to Chicago together right now. We will rent the Gary Stadium tonight, and fill it with workers, and then we will find out whether you are man enough to look them in the eye and repeat that contemptible performance."

Absolute silence descended upon the room when he finally paused for breath, and with his chin stuck out toward me rested his arms upon the table and waited for my reply. I was in panic. I was deathly afraid that a wrong word from me, spoken offhand in hot anger, might do great harm to the management position. And on one thing he was absolutely right. I certainly did not dare go to Gary and accept his challenge — though not for the reasons he stated. I knew that I had no chance to win an argument in that stadium, and that I would merely be giving him a nationwide forum which he needed badly. There was no chance whatever to advance our cause under those circumstances, and great risk that our position would be misrepresented and become distorted before the public. So I climbed down as skillfully as I could, and in a few restrained words declined to go.

One might think that this would have embittered our relationship, but nothing of the sort occurred. It had no more lasting effect than occurs when two old friends who are lawyers are engaged on opposite sides of a case and have a sharp altercation in front of a jury. This was a typical Phil Murray act, put on to impress his associates on his side of the table. I was very mad at the moment, but I too calmed down, and a half hour later we were kidding each other in the corridor as we walked out during an adjournment.

The reason why I came to believe that Phil had the same feeling toward me that I did toward him was this.

In the last bitter strike which he led before his death, he attacked one by one the salaries of the chief officers of the steel companies. I listened to him often in the privacy of my living room when he went on the air, and noticed that he never seemed to mention my name. Then one day a labor lawyer whom I knew called at my office, came in my room with an air of mystery about him, declined even to sit down, and said quickly, "I have a personal message for you. It is from Phil. He told me to say to you that he is tearing the other fellows apart about their salaries, but that he is not going to touch you." I wanted no favors from the CIO, yet I was genuinely moved by this — particularly since I had always seen to it that my salary was the lowest among all of the large companies.

Now Phil Murray is gone, and I mourn his passing. I fought him step by step, but out of our struggle there was born in my heart genuine affection for him.

10

❖ ❖
❖

W. Averell Harriman

I HAVE GREAT respect and admiration for Averell
Harriman. It so happens that he is a Democrat and
that I am a Republican, but that difference in party
affiliation has never for a moment impinged upon the
warmth of our personal relationship.

It is not always thus in our country, unhappily. I know
men in both parties who, when confronted with a question of public policy, ask immediately how the Democrats and the Republicans stand on it. If their party is
for it, so are they, without further argument. If the other
party proposed the idea, however, that is all that they
need to know. Ipso facto they are against it.

This is not intelligent behavior in a democracy. We
need more personal friendships that cross party lines, and
more independent judgments where citizens form their
opinions on public questions solely by thinking the
problems through for themselves. If when a man decides
on his own what is right he suddenly finds that this is

the view held by the opposite party, he must nevertheless stand fast for the right as he sees it, and make his
opinion clear to his friends.

I have had the privilege of knowing fairly intimately
important public figures in both parties, and I have
found no reliable index to their personal attributes
based upon party affiliation. I have watched them under
fire when charged with high responsibility, and in terms
of human strengths and weaknesses have found no way
to distinguish Democrats from Republicans. Regardless
of party, some are willful and impulsive, some are humble
and wise. Some are good team players, some intense
individualists. Some act first and tell their colleagues
later, while some seek counsel wherever it may be found.
So, Republican that I am, I have been proud of my
friendships on the other side of the aisle.

It was inevitable that Averell Harriman and I should
get to know one another. Much of his public service has
been in the area of foreign policy, and since that has
been my field of interest too, we have crossed each other's
paths many times. The thing that I have particularly
admired about him is this. He has a very special gift
which is rare among Americans, that of understanding
what it is that makes a foreigner behave as he does. When
he is in Pakistan he has an uncanny instinct for sensing
why the man across the table from him takes the position that he does, and he exhibits the same natural
shrewdness when he is in France or Russia, or any other
nation. The weakness of most of us Americans when
dealing with the national of another country is that

we treat him as though his reactions should be exactly the same as ours would be if we were in his place. This ignores the fact that he has centuries of mores and traditions behind him which are completely at variance with our own, and unless we can rise above this, and evaluate properly those mental and spiritual differences of his, we are likely to be guilty of serious errors in our bargaining. Averell Harriman possesses this gift to an extraordinary degree.

I first fell under his influence in Paris on the Fourth of July in 1948. That was the day when he became my boss, the day when I signed on as a member of his staff for the setting up of the Marshall Plan, having been persuaded to do this by his boss, my old friend Paul Hoffman. I was to be his consultant for steel and coal.

Unfortunately I had not yet made in my own life the adjustments in attitude of which I have just spoken. I knew nothing whatever of the foreign scene. This was just another business problem so far as I was concerned — a brief interlude in my life which had to be endured, and then I would be released to go back to my desk in my company. In fact, I had considerable doubt as to whether it was really fair to the company for me to take my steady hand off the wheel for even the few weeks that would be involved — though I was only a vice president at the time. All that I knew about the Marshall Plan was the fact that by accident I had heard General Marshall make his now famous address announcing it while I was attending my thirty-fifth class reunion at Harvard. This went in one ear and out the other, however, and left practically no trace. So when I reached Paris, here was my state of mind: I did not have the slightest idea what I was supposed to do, but whatever it was, I intended to do it crisply and go home.

All that I saw about me on that first mad day was chaos. I had just left a highly organized office where if I pushed a button someone answered. Here the plasterers were just finishing the walls, and the furniture was being moved in. There was no button to push, and if there had been, no one would have answered. There was only one telephone for six of us in the industrial section to use, and the operator was bilingual only in the sense that she spoke neither French nor English well.

All this confusion I could have lived with, but I jumped to the conclusion that it flowed from lack of precision thinking in the Marshall Plan itself. No one seemed to know what his job was, and I promptly blamed Ambassador Harriman for that. I wanted to know precisely what I was supposed to do at nine o'clock the next morning, so that I could get on with it. I wanted a well-typed document of instructions telling me precisely what my responsibilities were with respect to coal and steel, and setting up a series of report conferences with the Ambassador.

How wrong I was! Averell himself had but just arrived. He knew little more than I did. He was just as anxious to get the picture of what the Marshall Plan could hope to accomplish as I was, and the sole reason for my being there was to help him find out. My job was to get out into the industrial sections of Europe on my own initiative, and not keep running to him all of the time. He was tied to his desk, and I had to be his eyes and ears in the area assigned to me. Every important leader in Europe was pursuing him with hand extended, and had he been quintuplets he could not possibly have done all that was expected of him. How he managed to bring focus into our effort as soon as he did is a marvel to me now as I look back upon it, particularly now that I myself have had experience in government.

My mood of frustration soon yielded to better sense, however. As the weeks went along not only did we get enough chairs so that we could all sit down at the same time, plus competent secretaries, but my eyes began to open, and I felt the excitement of new challenge. After this came the deep inner satisfaction of feeling that I was playing a modest part in an undertaking of great historical significance. At the same time I began to understand my chief, and there began to form in my mind and heart the respect and affection which I now have for him.

At first I thought that he was not aggressive enough, not sufficiently tough in his attitude toward the surging throng of importunate people who besieged him constantly. But again I was wrong. Underneath that affable and almost gentle manner lay a will power that could be very firm indeed.

I remember one instance of this in particular because I was involved in it.

One of the most urgent problems facing the implementation of the Marshall Plan was the necessity for the reintegration of the economies of Germany and France, and my field of responsibility touched this because of the importance of both steel and coal in the recovery programs. The task was not easy because of the residual mistrust and animosity which persisted between these two recent enemies. Incredible as it seems, Germany had dared to face the combined strength of the principal industrial nations of the world without possessing a single important deposit of iron ore. Her steel industry and her entire massive fabric of war production had had to depend almost exclusively upon iron ore imported from Sweden. It was high time now that as the defeated belligerent she should resume giving some of that purchasing power to the French mines in Alsace-Lorraine. Conversely, the steel industry of northern France had been hard put to it when deprived of importations of coke made from coal mined in the Ruhr. If French costs were to come down, that situation also had to be reversed. Just where the American authority lay for carrying out these changes which so vitally affected the two countries simultaneously was not clear. General Lucius Clay was at the head of the American occupation forces in Germany, with his headquarters in Berlin, while Ambassador Harriman was in Paris as Paul Hoffman's deputy for the Marshall Plan, which dealt with Europe as a whole.

One day when I was attending a steel committee meeting at which the various countries were represented, one of the men from Luxemburg, whom I had come to know fairly intimately, beckoned to me as he passed me in the corridor and whispered to me in French, "Did you know that General Clay is going to raise the price of German coke to us and to the French tomorrow?" I was completely stunned by this news. To ask devastated France to raise her costs still further to help the defeated Nazis seemed to me the exact opposite of what the Marshall Plan was expected to do, yet knowing General Clay as I did I realized that I ought not to prejudge his case without hearing his reasons. "How do you know this?" I asked my friend. By way of reply he merely smiled a cryptic smile, said, "We Luxemburgers have long ears," and walked away.

I sensed a crisis, so I grabbed a cab, tore back to the office, and without stopping to ask permission burst into the Ambassador's private office, where I found him deep in conference with Paul Hoffman, who had just flown over, and with our new deputy, Bill Foster. My news hit them like a thunderclap. This was a real crisis. They saw it just as I had, but they were up to their eyes in another crisis which could not wait. Averell made up his mind instantly. Turning to me he said, "Clarence, this is very, very serious. I put you in charge. Take immediately in my name whatever steps you think are necessary, and have that coke price increase stopped until General Clay and I can get together and discuss it." This was language that I understood and was accustomed to. It was firm, decisive, and a clear delegation of authority.

But what to do? There was no time to lose, for the afternoon was already well advanced, and I left the room with my mind spinning. Suddenly I bethought myself of my old friend from Chicago, Bob Trier, who was in Paris as General Clay's liaison man with the various agencies located there. I had great respect for him. Because he had been born in Germany, our military people had rejected his offer of service during the war, but he persevered in his loyalty to the United States, and volunteered to serve with General Clay during the occupation.

He and I were always Bob and Clarence when we were together, but I wanted him to know that there was a crisis, and to have him on his guard, so when I put the telephone call through to him I began with, "Is this Mr. Trier?" Then when he inquired who was calling, I went on this way: "This is Mr. Randall. I am speaking for Ambassador Harriman. The Ambassador has reason to believe that General Clay proposes to raise the German coke price tomorrow. Kindly inform the General that the Ambassador asks that this not be done until the two of them have had an opportunity to discuss the matter together." I could almost hear Bob's heels click as he replied, "Very good, Mr. Randall. I understand, sir, and shall convey your message to General Clay at once."

That did it. Next day there came a message from the General saying that he had been giving some thought to raising the price of coke, and suggesting that he fly to Paris to discuss it with Averell. This was highly responsible behavior between two men of quality. The meeting was promptly held, face-to-face discussion cleared the air, the coke price was not increased, and

Washington never knew that there had been a crisis.

By September my tour of duty had ended, and I was free to go back to my desk in Chicago. I had visited all of the principal steel-making and coal-mining centers in the countries involved in the Marshall Plan, had met the leaders of those two industries, had discussed the problems with the appropriate officers of the various governments, and had laid before the Ambassador an outline of what I thought should be done.

When the time came for me to say goodbye to Averell, I was under considerable emotion. I had shaken off my businessman's veneer of self-assurance, and was deeply moved by what I had seen of the incredible responsibility which he and Paul Hoffman were bearing for the restoration of Europe. My respect was now warm with affection. In fact, the only real grievance that I still harbored against the Ambassador was that on the day when Emily arrived to join me — having come over against the advice of most of our friends, who earnestly believed that she would be in great personal danger because of the threat of invasion by Russia — he made me an hour late for dinner with her at Du Fruit Défendu by holding me in his office to clear some cables.

A year and a half later Emily and I were back in Paris, staying as always at the Crillon, because of its proximity both to the Embassy and to the Talleyrand Palace, where Averell had his office. One morning she asked me whether I was not going to drop by and pay my respects to him, but I said firmly that I was not. I explained impatiently to my inquiring wife that ambassadors were busy men, that they were daily besieged by name droppers and prestige seekers who wanted to go home and slip casually into conversation the remark, "By the way, I saw Averell in Paris," and that I refused to be guilty of such conduct.

Less than an hour later the phone rang in our room, and when I answered I recognized the voice instantly. It was that of one of Averell's secretaries, a most intelligent young lady who later became the wife of Boris Shishkin, the American labor leader. She said, "Hi, Mr. Randall! So you're ducking the boss! He knows you are in Paris, and he is unhappy that you have not been in to see him." I was completely astonished, and said, "How in the world did you perform this miracle?" "Oh, I have my ways," she replied with a laugh. "Do you want to know where else you have been in Europe?" I gasped again. "Never mind," she went on, "just please be in his office on Saturday afternoon at two o'clock."

When I arrived, Averell was alone, with not a paper on his desk. He had freed himself from every possible interruption, just to talk with me, and I was greatly touched. But this was just the beginning of my astonishment. He leaned back in his chair and began with clock-like precision a recapitulation of my earlier activity. It went like this: "When you left here a year and a half ago you handed me a memorandum of what you thought I should do about steel and coal in Europe. You said that I should undertake A, and B, and C, and D (still without a note in front of him). I want you to know that I did this about A, this about B, this about C, and

[84]

this about D." Not a detail of my report had escaped him, and not an item was unaccounted for as he went along.

I was overcome with humility, and deeply stirred by this painstaking recital of the planning in which I had been involved. It was a side of the Ambassador's nature that I had never seen before, and I was altogether inarticulate as I tried to acknowledge his kindness. In fact I did it so badly that I was relieved when he stopped the recapitulation and we drifted off into reminiscence.

But whenever I have thought of that Saturday afternoon since, my heart has always opened toward this man. He is a fine American. He has not always been fully understood by the American people, but in the end that is certain to be corrected.

11

✧ ✧
✧

Jean Monnet and the Common Market

HISTORY MOVES at times in a mysterious way to bury the past in the present. As a consequence, we are often under the false impression that what is more or less had to be, and that what we observe around us is the result of a natural process of evolution, untouched by human intervention.

The existence of the European Common Market proves how untrue that can be. That miracle of modern times sprang from the brain of just one man, Jean Monnet of France, and when measured against the residual animosities of the period immediately following the last war, it seems almost incredible.

I did not meet Monnet during my 1948 term of service in Paris under the Marshall Plan, but I learned a great deal about him. He was then engaged in developing the Plan Monnet, which dealt with the reconstruction of French industry. I worked very closely with his staff, and there can be no more revealing insight into a man's character than to find unfeigned admiration for him among his closest associates, such as I found with them. It was they who set up my schedule of steel-plant and coal-mine visitations, and who made it possible for me to meet the industrial leaders not only of France but of Belgium, Luxemburg, and Holland. It was not until later that I had the great privilege of knowing this extraordinary man himself.

The first bold step toward integrating the economy of Europe was the Schuman Plan for the establishment of a Coal and Steel Community which would cross national boundaries, reduce trade barriers, and stimulate production in those basic industries. The courageous announcement by which this revolutionary idea was first proposed was made on May 9, 1950, by M. Robert Schuman, the Foreign Minister of France. Every word of that history-making document was probably written by Jean Monnet, but that in itself was not enough. Fortunately for the world the brilliance of this mind was buttressed by the magnificent statesmanship of M. Schuman, who held the right government post at the right time.

By strange coincidence, I was in Paris on that very day, and looking back over the years now I am not proud of the fact that I gave little thought to the Schuman declaration as I read about it in the morning French papers. I was on pleasure bent at the time. Emily and I were about to embark upon an automobile trip to the north with our very dear friends and neighbors Pat and Hilpa Wood, and nothing else mattered.

Before the day was out, however, the seriousness of

it had been brought sharply home to me. By noon we reached Longwy, in the north of France, where one of my new friends, M. Tannery, who managed the steel plant there, gave a delightful luncheon for us in his home. The guests whom our gracious host had assembled to meet us were already there when we arrived. They were nearly all industrialists, and among them was Jean Raty, Chairman of the Board of M. Tannery's company, and several of his fellow directors.

They were in a high state of excitement when we entered the house, and the most animated conversation was going forward. They had just heard of the Schuman declaration. They were dumbfounded by it. They were highly indignant at the idea that the coal and steel industries of France and Germany should somehow be "pooled," and in evaluating now this first reaction of theirs, it must be remembered that Longwy was a border town, and that they had lived long years in the shadow of Hitler's military power. They were particularly disturbed that neither they nor their opposite numbers in the other companies had been consulted in advance. By now, if I were to see them again, I suspect that they would agree with me that had such consultations been held in advance by Schuman and Monnet, the resistance would have been so great that the declaration would never have been issued. The move had to be bold or not attempted at all.

I was the first American whom they had seen after the announcement, and knowing that I had had a government post, they poured vigorous protests into my ears, which I am bound to say gave me serious concern as we started on our way again after lunch.

A few night later we were in Brussels, and again the Schuman Plan pursued me. We had a delightful dinner at the residence of our Chicago friends John and Grace Nuveen. John was at that time the head of our economic assistance program for Belgium. The guest of honor was M. Eyskens, the Prime Minister of Belgium, and once more this new and astonishing declaration by the Foreign Minister of France became the dominant theme of the conversation. He also knew of my government relationships, and probed me skillfully, trying to uncover what I thought of it. I did the same with him, but we were both on our guard. He knew precisely what was involved. He had been a professor of economics at Louvain University, and saw at once both the subtleties and the complexities of this new concept. He knew that there was no escape for him, and that he must think it through at once, for it was certain to be the most controversial subject facing his government in the immediate future. He gave me no sure hint as to his ultimate position, but paid generous tribute to the courageous leadership of the French Foreign Minister, while at the same time pointing out that this was not a plan, but an invitation to a conference for the purpose of jointly creating a plan.

As our trip came to an end and we turned back toward home, I could not put this totally unexpected development out of my mind. For months I thought of little else when I had time to reflect about the situation in Europe. The more I weighed M. Schuman's declaration, and the more I read of the international conferences that were held concerning it, the more I was torn between anxiety and admiration. On the one hand I feared that this might be the first step toward a giant cartel in which prices, wages, and profits would all be controlled in a planned economy, and that it might thus lead all Europe into socialism. On the other hand I could not forget the work that I had been engaged in. The purpose of the Marshall Plan was to make Europe strong that the United States might be secure. Economic unity in Europe would greatly advance that objective, and would provide a basis upon which political unity might later be developed as a barrier to a westward thrust by the Soviets.

No one at that time could possibly guess how it would all come out. The man in the street cheered everywhere, and Germany spoke up promptly with unqualified endorsement, but the other governments backed and filled. Britain, under the Labor Party and Mr. Attlee, were both for and against the proposal for several days, and then turned it down. Their official public statements rather left the suggestion that there would be time enough to discuss the pooling of coal and steel on an international basis when the other countries had attained the social maturity found in England, where basic industry had been "rationalized" — meaning subjected to socialist control.

In September of 1950 I was back again in Paris, this time with Paul Hoffman, for whom I had once more undertaken a short assignment in connection with the Marshall Plan. At noon after our arrival, the staff gave a small luncheon for us, and it was there that I first came to know Jean Monnet, being introduced by Paul Hoffman himself.

I was thrilled to meet this genius about whom I had heard so much, and who was now so widely recognized as the spiritual and intellectual leader of the reconstruction effort in France. He fascinated me as, in perfect English, he outlined his broad philosophy in general and the Schuman Plan in particular. He said that the French government in issuing the Schuman declaration did not regard coal and steel as important in themselves, but that those industries merely provided the best medium by which they might reach their prime objective, which was the breaking down of national barriers. I am bound to confess that I was dismayed by this statement, for I was still active in the steel business myself, and I felt that he did not much care what happened to my chosen industry so long as what he did advanced the cause of a United States of Europe. But I could not resist his magnetism. Never in my life have I been so completely captivated by a new personality as I was that day, and to cap the climax he invited me to come and lunch privately with him as soon as I could.

On that occasion, I surrendered completely. I was accompanied by my Chicago friend Tom Kearney, the well-known management consultant who was working with me, and Monnet was flanked by my younger new friend, Albert Denis, of the French government.

Monnet's office was on the left bank. We were promptly received, shown along a winding corridor and up a very perpendicular and narrow staircase to a small and austere little dining room, where, before an open fire that was almost too hot for comfort, a spotless table was set. The food was simple but marvelously prepared. There was only a token glass of wine, which surprised me a bit since our host's family business had been cognac, but he said to me, "We do our work here on water."

Here was a man who would have passed unnoticed in any company had it not been for the extraordinary power of his mind. Short of stature and impassive of countenance, he made no conscious effort to command attention. There was no lifting of the hand to ask for silence, no pounding of the table to drive home a point. His attitude was that of a thoughtful listener seeking wisdom from others — until he quietly chose the occasion to speak. Then everything changed. Immediately he was master of the situation; not because he was an important person, but because what he said was so well conceived and so well said that it was not open to challenge.

The clarity and power of his thought was a joy to experience. His English was not only correct, but effortless. Occasionally we lapsed into French if one of his associates wished to make a point and did not quite trust himself in English, but language did not seem to matter in the midst of ideas. I was in the presence of one of the most facile minds I had ever encountered, and one of the most honest. My doubts disappeared when I found that he was in complete accord with me that for a vital economy industry must be constantly policed by vigorous competition. It was his creed that the function of business is to serve the public, and that private agreements which limit the carrying out of that obligation must be prohibited. Otherwise the public will be driven to protecting itself through the nationalization of industry. I was deeply moved by our talk, and left with the conviction that the shaping of the destiny of Europe toward economic integration was in strong hands.

By August of 1952 the Schuman Plan had become my consuming passion, so back to Europe I went again, this time as a private citizen, but with the full approval of the new Eisenhower administration in Washington, and with the best of advance briefing. I wanted to see again the leaders of the steel industry in the various countries whom I had met earlier, and to urge them to take two positions in public: first, to resist asking the United States to advance capital to the new High Authority of the Coal and Steel Community; and secondly, to oppose all efforts to introduce restrictive practices and other cartel manifestations into the new organization.

I remember this trip especially because of a hilarious incident that occurred in London. My friend C. R. (Mike) Wheeler, of the steel industry of Great Britain, gave a luncheon for me at the Savoy Hotel, to which he invited a dozen or so of the top-ranking civil servants from the British government who had been following the progress of the Schuman Plan. From the moment we were seated at table we talked of nothing else. By this time England had crossed the Rubicon. When the Labor government rejected the Coal and Steel Community, barriers against unity of action were erected which were to plague Europe for long years to come.

Because the occasion was light in tone, I began to spoof my British comrades. The Coal and Steel Community had just established its headquarters in Luxemburg, and I said, "What will your contacts be with this new supranational sovereignty? Will you enter into diplomatic relationships with it, and appoint an ambassador?"

There was considerable hemming and hawing at this, and I could see that I had touched on a sore spot. Obviously they had been asking themselves the same question, and had arrived at no satisfactory answer. Someone hesitantly suggested that they might perhaps send an observer over. I sensed that many of them already feared that their failure to join the Community promptly, and with enthusiasm, might create great difficulties for England in the future.

I kept pressing my point home with mock seriousness, and finally said, "Well, at least tell me this. What are your purposes and objectives with respect to the Schuman Plan?"

This was too much, and one of my listeners (he came to be widely known in England later) exploded with, "I'll tell you what our purposes and objectives are. Do you know your Milton?"

"Of course I know my Milton," I answered, still playing the game.

"Well, then," he ejaculated, "our purpose and objective is to creep and intrude, and climb into the fold." And this Britain has been trying to do ever since, without success.

The final bit of personal involvement for me in connection with European integration occurred in September of 1956. I was back in London, this time as a member of the White House staff, with foreign economic policy as my field of responsibility. My friend Win Brown, a member of the foreign service who has had an exceptionally distinguished career, was at that time the economic officer at our embassy in London. The Common Market was by then getting under way. The Conservative Party had been returned to power, and they were struggling with the dilemma created by the earlier rejection of the Schuman Plan. Harold Macmillan was Chancellor of the Exchequer. To my surprise, Win said that the Chancellor had heard that I was coming over, and had expressed a desire to see me. I replied that it was part of my code never to see officers of foreign governments, since in my opinion that was the job of the State Department, and not of the White House, but he replied, "Well, I am giving a little dinner for you tonight at my club, and if he drops by I guess you can't refuse to see him."

And that was precisely what happened. He did stop by, and as it turned out the timing of his call was dramatic. Debate had been on in Parliament all that day over Suez, and the final vote was to come at midnight. Nevertheless, Chancellor Macmillan came at eight and stayed until nine-twenty. He did not take dinner, since he had to go back to Parliament, but he insisted that the rest of us seat ourselves at table, and go ahead, which we did.

At the outset, I formed a very poor impression of this distinguished gentleman. I thought that he looked and acted like the Englishman whom we caricature in our funny papers.

But just before he left, I saw the real Macmillan, and my opinion changed instantly. He asked me if he might say a word to me privately, and when we were alone he launched into the most enthusiastic endorsement of the concept of the economic integration of Europe and the philosophy underlying the Common Market. I was tremendously impressed. I discovered that he had a profound grasp of all phases of the problem, and an almost spiritual fervor in support of it.

At the end he put his hand on my shoulder, and said earnestly, "Remember this! The Common Market wins or loses depending upon whether President Eisenhower publicly gives it his blessing."

As I flew home across the Atlantic that interview and those final words of the Chancellor kept coming back to my mind. President Eisenhower was in the midst of his campaign for reelection, and immediately upon my return, I did something impulsively. I knew what the President's thinking was on this subject. He believed fervently in the economic integration of Europe, because he saw it as the first step toward the political unity of purpose which he so passionately felt was required as a matter of our national security vis-à-vis Russia. I also knew that he was speaking somewhere nearly every day. So I drafted two paragraphs expressing the hope that the Common Market might succeed, and gave them to his personal staff, on the off chance that he might find them suitable for use in public.

Not long after that I took a short vacation trip to North Dakota, and on one lovely moonlight evening when there was just a touch of frost in the air, I was driving along a remote country road. I had the car radio turned on and was listening to the news. Suddenly I was electrified. There was the voice of President Eisenhower making an address in Miami, and over the air came my two paragraphs, with not a word changed. He was giving the Common Market his blessing, and was saying to the world what I had often heard him say in private.

My heart was very full — and it still is whenever I think of that evening.

12

❖ ❖
❖

A Lady from Great Britain

WAR IS A disruptive force. It bursts through
tradition with all the explosive power of nuclear
fission, and nowhere is this more evident than in the
processes of government.

In Great Britain, for example, the last war emanci-
pated women. The doors of opportunity were suddenly
flung open to them so that they might display their
quality in the carrying of great responsibility, and the
record was spectacular.

When the men rushed off to take their posts in the
trenches and on the beachheads, Churchill's staff in
desperation turned to Oxford, Cambridge, and the
other fine universities to find feminine replacements.

It was thus that Miss Elizabeth Ackroyd entered the
British government, and today there is no finer career
officer in any nation. She has held in succession a wide
variety of posts, bringing to each extraordinary talent,

but her first was in steel, and that was how I came to know her.

In 1948 when I was suddenly catapulted into Paris to join Averell Harriman's Marshall Plan staff as his consultant for steel and coal, I had but one desire, and that was to get the job over with as fast as possible. I wanted action.

So when I heard that there was a new entity known as the Organization for European Economic Cooperation I dashed over to its headquarters, and asked whether there was such a thing as a steel committee.

Sure enough there was, and when I plunged ahead, and asked whether I could meet the chairman, the genial officer who had taken me in charge said, "Certainly, sir. Come with me." He led me down the hall, into an office, and there introduced me to a young lady about the age of my oldest daughter — Miss Elizabeth Ackroyd.

I was a bit nonplussed, but there I was, and there she was, so stumbling ahead, and unable to think of anything better to do, I asked the lady whether she could come over to the Crillon Hotel and have tea with me that afternoon. She came, and thus began a friendship which has steadily deepened through the years, and one which has meant a great deal both to me and to my family.

To watch her chair the meetings of the steel committee was a unique experience. Here was a young woman just out of the university, presiding daily over sessions where not only was she the only lady in the

room, but where the participants were senior industrialists from every Marshall Plan country, all of whom
were accustomed to bearing a great responsibility at
home. Yet it worked, and worked amazingly well. The
men around that table came to have the same respect
for their chairman that I did.

Here was her secret. She was a person of great charm.
Never for a moment did she cease to be feminine, never
did she cease to be a lady. Never did an undignified
word pass her lips, but she understood the workings of
the masculine mind so infallibly that men forgot that
she was a woman. They gladly accepted her as their
boss. She made them toe the mark, and they liked it.

She made me toe the mark, too. She made it clear to
me that when meetings were held I was to be an observer, and not a participant. I was to be seen, and not
heard. This was highly responsible conduct, but not
easy, for this was a time when all Europe was reaching
for our money, and when we of the American staff
were being avidly cultivated on all sides. Some of my
colleagues were at times a bit overzealous in telling
Europeans what to do, but the right approach, looking
toward the future, was for the Europeans to do the
planning and deciding, and for us to support their proj-
ects when we felt that we could. So Miss Ackroyd said
simply and quietly at the first meeting which I attended,
"We are happy to have the American observer with us
today. Should he have an inquiry to make, if he will
be good enough to present it to the chairman, I shall

be glad to determine whether in my judgment it should be presented to the meeting."

She did me the honor of assigning me a seat on her right at the conference table, and I greatly admired her skill as a presiding officer. Once when the Belgian representative asked her a question in French, she replied instantly and confidently in English, and when I asked her later how she came to have such a complete reply ready on the instant, she smiled her modest but winning smile, and said with a twinkle in her eye, "I knew what he was going to ask before he asked it."

As of 1948 neither she nor I could have foreseen the impact which those meetings were destined to have, not only upon reconstruction of production units, but upon the political integration of Europe. The short-term objective of putting the basic industry of steel back on its feet was brilliantly accomplished, but in terms of history here was where a new atmosphere for the mutual sharing of problems on a working level was first created for modern Europe. The friendships formed around that table became firm for all time. Men from many nations, each a leader at home, came to understand and rely upon one another.

As I look back upon those sessions now, I come to the sober conclusion that it was from the sessions of that steel committee, so competently chaired by Elizabeth Ackroyd, that the concept of the European Coal and Steel Community came into being, just as it is equally clear to me that the ultimate design for the Common Market originated in the Steel Community.

So I say that few ladies have had the opportunity to influence history that came to Elizabeth Ackroyd, and few have measured up so magnificently.

13

✧ ✧
✧

Alfred M. Gruenther

FEW AMERICANS have achieved the high standard of continuous and dedicated service to our country that has been maintained throughout his entire life by Al Gruenther, and what is more, few have displayed such an amazing diversity of gifts.

From West Point on, his career in the army took him steadily up and up until he became first Chief of Staff for SHAPE, and finally Supreme Allied Commander in Europe. He won decoration after decoration, but no doubt the one of which he is most proud is the Distinguished Service Medal with two Oak Clusters. Then when, with the relentless advance of the years, the time came for him to retire from the military service, he made a characteristically bold and unselfish personal decision. Many large corporations were knocking at his door with attractive offers of positions of great prestige, coupled with high salaries, but he turned them all down, and chose instead to become head of the American Red

Cross. Again duty had called, and he made up his mind that here was his best opportunity for continuing to serve his country.

But what not everyone knows is that in the midst of the complex responsibilities which he bore, both in war and in peace, he never once lost his irrepressible sense of humor. Many an impasse has been eased by his sparkling wit and infectious smile, yet this side of his nature was always under full control. He could clown with the clowns, or be wise with the wise, whichever was the order of the day. He enlivened every group in which he participated. This was in part because he laughed easily himself, and could make others laugh, but also because he had a rare talent for keeping a conversation general instead of letting it degenerate into a series of unrelated dialogues. Above all, he listened just as well as he talked, which is unusual for a forceful leader.

But he could be deadly in earnest, too. In January of 1956 I was back in Paris. I was on my way out to Ankara in connection with my second mission to Turkey, and the General was kind enough to arrange a briefing session for us at his SHAPE headquarters.

When we reached there we were impressed with the buildings because they were so simple and austere. Not an unnecessary dollar had been spent.

The General conducted the briefing himself, starting precisely as scheduled at 11:15 A.M., and stopping at 12:25. His capacity for brilliant repartee was bridled. He was crisp and orderly in his presentation as he took us thoughtfully through the problems of our relationships with Turkey, and what he said had all the freshness of approach that it would have had if this had been his first briefing session on Turkey, instead of his fiftieth. We were greatly awed by it all. The matters which he discussed with us were so complex, and the relationships with our allies so delicate, that we wondered how one man could face up to them with such radiant leadership.

That evening, however, I saw the other Al Gruenther, and learned that it is dangerous to enter a room on a social occasion when he is present without having one's tongue at the ready.

We were both guests at a small and delightful dinner given for us in the home of George Perkins, who was then our ambassador to NATO. The table was magnificent, the cuisine perfection, and the guests wisely chosen. I was seated on the right of my hostess, Mrs. Perkins, and the General was on her left. His greeting to me went something like this: "Hello, hot shot! It must be wonderful to do nothing but go around the world attending dinners." He beamed raillery like that at me all evening, and I was hard put to it to hold up my end, but I did manage to do so once. The month was January, and he knew that I would retire from my company the following April 1. He made so many good-natured gibes about the weary old men who were compelled to retire from business that I finally said, "Well, at least we are not like the old soldiers; we die," and the guests howled.

Al Gruenther was at his very best, however, as a leg puller. In fact, in that catagory I have never known his equal. More than once I have been his victim, and always I have loved his ribbing, because it is so superbly done and never has a trace of malice. His nature is too generous for that.

The best time ever was the following.

I was back once more in Paris in September of 1956, in the course of my White House work in the field of foreign economic policy. I had asked the General if I might have a conference with him, and he had replied, "I will have no part in your black art of economics, but I want you to come out for a thinking, talking session."

Late one afternoon, accompanied by my colleagues, I drove out to his quarters, as distinguished from his office. He was then Supreme Allied Commander, and lived in a modest-sized but beautiful old chateau in a little village which had another distinguished resident — Maurice Chevalier.

Measuring the distance carefully in my mind, I governed the speed of our car so that I might arrive at his front door at precisely the time he had indicated. I knew that he would expect that of me. We were received by members of the General's staff, including four-star General Schuyler, and four-star General Decker, but to my astonishment General Gruenther was not there. Knowing how precision-minded he was, I could only assume that a sudden crisis had arisen. The explanation given to me was that he had unexpectedly been detained at his headquarters by a delegation from Norway.

Actually the whole thing was a gag in order that the General might later make a dramatic entrance, and they were all in on it.

About ten minutes later he strode in, gave me a nod and a quick handshake, and exploded: "Boy, am I ever burned!" I tried to imagine what new contretemps had arisen in NATO, but he went on: "I have never been so mad and disgusted in my life. Waiter, bring me a double Scotch! I need it badly." (Actually, he never touched it after it came.)

The atmosphere was so charged with electricity that none of us dared speak, but finally General Schuyler seemed to gather sufficient courage, and he said in a shocked voice, "Al, what's the matter? I have never seen you like this before in my life."

Then pounding the table so hard with his fist that he almost knocked it over, Al said, "What is this country of ours coming to? The tripe they print in the magazines these days!" At that he began to read from something which he was holding in his hand, pausing after each sentence or two to condemn the utter stupidity of the author.

Suddenly I recognized that he was reading from an article of mine on the subject of retirement which the New York *Times* had just printed in its Sunday magazine. The day of the week was Wednesday, and I had not yet seen it myself, for it had been published only the preceding Sunday, after I had left the United States. In spite of the fact that he was up to his eyes in work, he had taken the time and pains gleefully to lay this trap for me. Actor that he was, he knew perfectly well that he was himself on the verge of retirement from the military service, and in his serious moments he agreed completely with my conclusions. He accepted and lived with the philosophy that this personal crisis must be taken in stride with no backward look, that the door to the past must be closed, and that the satisfactions for the years ahead must be sought in new challenge.

A friendship formed with such a man is in fact like an old soldier — it never can die. It does not even fade away.

To prove this, let me quote the final paragraph of a letter which Al Gruenther wrote me recently when he learned that I was convalescing from a second coronary thrombosis.

Here is what it said:

"Now please take your pills, and don't get excited about anything. The American Red Cross will take care of the problems of the world while you are in the hospital!"

14

❖ ❖
❖

Kwame Nkrumah

LIKE SO MUCH else that has happened to me in my life, my sudden plunge into the problems of emerging Africa was totally unpremeditated, and of all the adventures which I have now had on that exciting continent none have been more colorful, none more stimulating, than those that came to me in the course of my activities with respect to Ghana. Best of all has been the privilege of coming to know intimately President Nkrumah, and of trying to penetrate the inner mysteries of his mind and spirit.

Here is a man who by any standard must be recognized as one of the most significant leaders in the New Africa, yet but few Americans have endeavored thoughtfully to examine his personal philosophy, or to evaluate objectively the contributions which he has made to the welfare of his people. It is much simpler to blast him with a condemnatory epithet such as "that Commie over there," and then to hurry on to more important matters. I sometimes wonder whether like-minded men and women who were living in Europe toward the close of the eighteenth century similarly dismissed Thomas Jefferson and others of our innovating ancestors shortly after the American Revolution. Certain it is that if Nkrumah possesses all of the vices which many of his critics in the United States assert that he does when denouncing him the situation must in part be our fault. He lived among us for ten years, and since no one denies that he is possessed of a powerful mind, it must be concluded that he had before him the image of both our good qualities and our bad ones when he shaped his own life.

He is called Osagyefo by his people, which means something close to Redeemer, and many Americans jeer at that. On the one hand, this may be gross vanity and affectation on his part, as these critics assert, or on the other, it may merely be the impenetrable mystery of the African soul which moves his people even against his wish to bestow that title upon him. In Liberia, President Tubman has built for himself a marble palace, though his country is still poverty stricken, but that is the way his people want it. Their intense nationalism finds gratification in the belief thus visibly expressed that he is just as great a man as the President of the United States.

One thing I know. I shall never fully understand the motivations of Kwame Nkrumah, or the inner workings of his mind, but by the same token I am quite sure that he has the same difficulty with me. We are divided by the barriers of centuries of traditions and behavior patterns, and we cannot expect suddenly to set all that aside and enter into full rapport. I cannot even pronounce his name with confidence. Some Americans who ought to know call it Enkrumah, while others with equal assurance say Nuhkrumah. I have listened attentively when I have heard his name spoken by his close associates, but I am still in doubt. The reason is that the sound coming from an African mouth and throat is bound to be different from that which comes from mine. This much, however, is clear to me. When I am in the presence of the chief executive of the new nation called Ghana, I am fascinated by him.

I first arrived in the capital city of Accra on Palm Sunday, 1958, just a year after Ghana had become an independent state. Nkrumah was then Prime Minister under a British Governor-General, Earl Listowel, for the country did not become a republic with him as its President until July 1, 1960. The rains were due any day, but my luck held almost to the end of my stay, and outside the sun had all of its tropical brilliance. I was amazed at the physical comfort of the new Ambassador Hotel, and greatly intrigued by the spectacle outside my hotel window where a crowd of African men kept milling through the city park taking their Sunday strolls. Some wore Western clothes, while some had the "cover cloth," which consisted of yards of fabric in brilliant color which they were continuously clutching and adjusting.

Nearly everyone whom I know speaks of Ghana as a

"new" country, and so it is in terms of political independence, but the image which that word creates in the mind of one who has not seen Africa is not a true one. The Gold Coast, as the country was known before independence, is older than the United States, and Accra, its capital, is older by far than my city of Chicago. The first Europeans to come there were the Portuguese, who reached the country in 1471 in the course of their expansion along the whole coast of West Africa. They promptly developed a profitable gold trade, but that was their undoing, for it aroused the envy and cupidity of other European countries, and they were driven out. Flocking in came the British, the French, the Flemish, the Dutch, and the Danes, all of whom kept on with the gold trade, but added slaves as an export commodity. Eventually the Gold Coast became one of the chief sources for slaves that were shipped to the United States as well as to Europe, and many of our Negro families today had their origins there.

The Danes confined their activities to the area near Accra, but there they left an imperishable mark in the form of Christiansborg Castle, which they built, and which stands by the sea. It is still a magnificent structure, yet it was erected in 1730, when Chicago's skyline had nothing to mark it except a string of Indian wigwams near the mouth of the river, where the Chicago *Tribune* Tower now stands.

It was in Christiansborg Castle that I made my first call of courtesy upon the Prime Minister. Now that he is President he has left the castle, which was inconveniently located at some distance from the city, and has both his residence and his administrative office at Flagstaff House, near the center of the modern part of Accra. I am told that he moved not only to have this more accessible location, but to escape the noise of the daily pounding of the surf on the rocks below the castle.

Even in 1958, Nkrumah was already the most talked about man in Africa south of the Sahara, and I am bound to say that the impression which he made upon me was a highly favorable one. His manner was altogether simple and unaffected, and we talked easily and pleasantly about the United States. He had come here at the age of twenty-two and had spent ten years. His memories were obviously pleasant ones, and in that critical period it was reassuring to sense in his attitude genuine affection for our country. His command of English was excellent, but, like many Africans, he has an occasional thickness of accent which can be baffling. I am told that in the Ivory Coast, which is an adjoining country, the African has less accent in speaking French than the Ghanaian in speaking English. It is thought that this is because French is spoken forward in the mouth, while English requires sounds formed in the back of the throat which are difficult for Africans.

I next saw this new African leader in the United States, when in July of 1958, while he was still Prime Minister, he came to this country on a state visit. My first glimpse of him was at a formal dinner given for him in Washington, but I was seated a long way from the salt, as the British say (and strangely enough, so was

Under Secretary of State Christian Herter), so that I saw little of what went on. I remember, however, how magnificent Vice President Nixon was as he gave the toast to the Queen. He had a very special gift on such occasions. I used to know by heart the familiar platitudes about the ties that bind two nations together, which are so often used, but what the Vice President said that evening was not only beautiful English, but it impressed everyone as coming straight from the heart.

I remember vividly one sentence spoken to me on that occasion by Sir Robert Jackson, who was the distinguished husband of Barbara Ward, and who had done so much for Ghana in his capacity of financial adviser to Nkrumah for development. We were talking about the difficulty which a man from one of the older nations has in getting fully inside an African, and the fact that in a new nation this is accentuated because the people live so intensively the thrilling adventure of their new independence that they do not readily receive ideas which are unrelated to their present experience. He said, "Never forget that in Ghana this is 1777."

A few days later the Prime Minister came to Chicago, and by virtue of that visit a sudden atmosphere of tension descended upon Emily and me when, with the guidance of the State Department, we gave a dinner for him in our home in Winnetka.

We had many problems, the first of which was security. The Secret Service wanted me to bring my guest out to our home in a limousine which they would provide and to have a motorcycle police escort ahead and behind, but I demurred. I said that my chauffeur and I made that run every night in my own car, and that business as usual was the safest course. My real reason was that if I came roaring into our peaceful village with a police escort, I would never be able thereafter to live it down.

But there was one slip. My next-door neighbor, to whom I was devoted, was the late Holman D. Pettibone, one of Chicago's finest citizens. We had cut a path through the trees and bushes that separated our houses, and often of an evening he came over unannounced for a chat. He did just that on this night, not knowing that anything was going on, and as he strolled along the path a security agent rose up out of the bushes and grabbed him. This he held over me for a long, long time.

Once we were inside, the first thing Nkrumah wanted to do was look around my house, and this he proceeded to do from cellar to garret. My generous wife even permitted me to commit the grossest sin of suburban life, which was to take him out into the kitchen at the very time when preparations for dinner were getting under way. The one thing which seemed most to arouse his curiosity was the type of steel window frames which we had installed. They open outward in a vertical position. He asked me where I had bought them, and when I told him that they had been imported from Great Britain, he asked for the name of the manufacturer. This I sent on to him afterwards, and I later learned that he had ordered duplicates and installed them in his summer home in the mountains north of Accra.

Before the dinner, which did not include ladies, Emily had a gay talk with him, in which she gave him sound advice as to what sort of present he should take home from America to his new wife.

The guests that evening included four Ghanaians, and five of my Chicago friends. There was no protocol whatever, not even place cards at the table. The conversation was completely relaxed, and we had the most direct interplay of ideas in an atmosphere that was always friendly. My friends were as fascinated by Nkrumah as I had been, and he said one thing which no one of us who was present will ever forget. It was this: "Wherever I go in your country, I hear people say that we in Ghana are not ready to govern ourselves. But, who are you to decide for another man when he is ready to govern himself? What does freedom mean? To me it means that each man decides that question for himself. In fact, it is my belief that a man has the right even to be misgoverned if he so elects." I could think of no good answer to make to that statement that night, and I have never been able to think of one since.

Thereafter Ghana was often in my thoughts as I read of its progress, particularly when on July 1, 1960, the country became a republic, with Nkrumah as its President. Then suddenly it was back in my life again when, in the fall of 1961, President Kennedy asked me to be his representative in connection with pending negotiations that dealt with a proposal for the construction of a dam across the Volta River. On this project hinged the economic future of Ghana. Completion of the dam would not only provide abundant electric power for the small industries which were so urgently needed in that new country, but would make possible the acceptance of an offer from American private investors, led by the Kaiser interests, to build there a large plant for the smelting of bauxite into aluminum.

I flew out to Accra during the last week in October, and the high spot of my visit was the conference which I had with Nkrumah. We were absolutely alone, with no staff on either side. Never have I talked straighter from the shoulder than I did that day, yet when I left I felt certain that there had been no impairment of our friendship, which I believed was deep and genuine on both sides.

Our conversation laid the foundation for the later consideration of the Volta project by President Kennedy. Once more I was impressed by the subtlety of this remarkable man's mind, and by the charm of his manner. I was touched that he began our meeting on a personal note by recalling most vividly the details of the dinner in our home and asking most graciously for Emily.

Next day I drove out to the site of the proposed dam, accompanied by two men of whom I had become very fond, our ambassador, Francis Russell, and Sir Robert Jackson. The countryside was magnificent — broad plains heading up into high forest-covered hills of majestic outlines. And the Ghanaian people were simply delightful — always laughing, always waving, and always tender with their children. We were on fine blacktop roads all the way, and we never saw another car. In fact, my spirits rose so high that I said to my companions, "I don't understand Americans. Why do they always choose to visit just those countries that have a past, instead of occasionally some that have a future? Look at that landscape! Could anything be more heavenly? And think of it! We have had this whole countryside to ourselves today!" That turned out to be a laugh, for we learned later that Osagyefo, as a matter of security for me, had closed that whole road for the entire day to all traffic except our car.

Then we went on to the site of the dam itself. It is called Akosombo, which means place where the stone is worshipped, or place of the river god. A covered observation platform had been built at exactly the right spot. The view was spectacular beyond words, for the whole great valley of the Volta River, running far to the north, lay before us. A luncheon table in excellent taste had been spread for us, and I could not help but wonder where in the United States this could have been so well done in so remote an area.

I came home with a whole new sequence added to my gallery of happy memories, made my report to the President, and took it for granted that my assignment was finished, but that was not to be. In December he asked me to go back once more for a further meeting with President Nkrumah on the subject of the Volta dam, and I accepted with enthusiasm.

The time schedule was snug. I received the telephone call on Wednesday, and was in the air on my way to Accra by Friday night. I had to be there by Saturday noon, and arrived precisely on the dot.

Taking our ambassador with me, I reached Flagstaff House as rapidly as I could, and promptly found myself seated once more face to face with Nkrumah on the large divan in his office. He listened with the most earnest attention while I said forcefully the things that I had come to say. He was unequivocal in his acceptance of the suggestions that I made, and I was completely satisfied with his attitude. I felt that we had come as close to complete understanding as is possible for men of such divergent backgrounds.

So far as my work was concerned, it was now finished, but adventure was still to come. The next day was Sunday, and that was a big day for Accra. Ghana was to play Nigeria in soccer for the championship of all Africa, and Osagyefo did me the honor of inviting me to be his special guest.

I was in a high state of anticipation when I arrived at the residence of Ambassador Russell to drive with him in his car to Flagstaff House, but, as so often happens with us amateur diplomats, I failed him badly in my observance of protocol. I was in my shirt sleeves. It was a warm day and this was a soccer game. I had not seen a jacket since I arrived. The startled Ambassador quickly set me right, however, and said that I must have one. There was not time to go back to my hotel, so he loaned me one of his, and I wore it all afternoon, in spite of the fact that the sleeves were three inches too long.

President Nkrumah greeted me at his residence, and he and I transferred ourselves to his Rolls-Royce. Then we set off down the main boulevard, preceded not only by a heavy police escort, but by a sound truck which was blaring out to the watching public the slogans of his political party.

When we reached the new athletic stadium, which had been built at the time of independence, forty thousand screaming Africans rose to their feet in a frenzy of welcome to their hero. We then were driven slowly around the running track. I found myself in the novel posture of having to raise my hand on my side of the car in response to the plaudits of the multitude whenever he did on his.

The game itself was thrilling, and Osagyefo, who was an old soccer player from his days at Lincoln University in this country, coached me on the fine points. To complete this as the day of days, Ghana won 5 to 2, and when the final whistle blew, and victory was secure, a roar of exultation rose from the crowd which shook the stadium to its foundations.

Nkrumah then led me down to the field, where one by one we shook hands with the players, congratulating them on their sportsmanship, and with the officials, complimenting them on their meticulous fairness. Then suddenly there was a burst of music from the band, and out of the corner of my eye I saw Osagyefo stiffen into a military salute. I imitated him instinctively, but I did not learn until later that this was the Ghanaian national anthem, which I had never heard before.

Finally we left, going once more slowly around the track while the audience cheered, and the mounted officers sat their horses in respectful salute. But when we were back on the highway, and the sounds of the crowd were subsiding behind us, he brought me back from my dream world with a very down-to-earth comment. He said, "You know, we have a tough problem here. We haven't got enough parking space for cars here at the stadium." Such is primitive Africa!

Just before I was scheduled to fly back to New York this unusual man sent me a very perceptive gift. How he knew that my passion was bird watching I cannot imagine, but when I opened the package which he sent me, I found that it contained a rare set of the classic work on the birds of West Africa, bearing a very friendly inscription from my host.

Throughout my various adventures in Ghana my one regret had been that Emily had not been with me to share them. I was anxious for her to see this colorful country about which I had said so much. Finally the opportunity came in October of 1962, when, on a trip which we took together out to South Africa, we were able to stop over in Accra for a few days.

The result was inevitable. Overnight she became as enthusiastic as I had been.

We devoted the first day, of course, to another pilgrimage to Akosombo to see how the Volta dam was coming. In doing so we first drove east to Tema, skirting for miles a lovely beach where a gentle surf was breaking. My objective was to see the new ocean port which now, for the first time in history, gave Ghana full access to the sea for its commerce. Nature has given West Africa mixed blessings. It is richly endowed with natural resources, but has very few good harbors. When I first saw Accra in 1958, the city could be served only by ships which anchored dangerously in the open roadstead and transferred their cargoes to small boats. These were then rowed ashore by Ashanti oarsmen who pulled their long sweeps in unison to the rhythm of their native songs. Curiously enough, though this was their trade, these men came from the northern part of the country. Now all this was gone, and here at Tema was a completely modern installation of breakwater, docks, unloading cranes, and warehouses.

At Akosombo we were the guests of the Kaiser organization, which was engineering the project, and their hospitality was very kind. We lunched in the delightful small hotel which was built to serve that area, and the genial proprietor, whom I had known earlier, graciously gave us his own private dining room, which looked right out at the Volta River and the magnificent mountain scenery in the background. The coffer dams were nearly finished, there was intense activity everywhere, and I was thrilled to find that this great project with which I had been associated at its inception was now in full swing. On the way back, I stopped to photograph a cocoa tree, and learned from our driver that cocoa, which is the base upon which the economy depends for earning foreign exchange, was first introduced into Ghana from Fernando Po, an island in the Gulf of Guinea, by a man named Tetteh Quarshe. Few men have done as much for a country by a single act.

I had hoped that on this trip to Ghana I might be free from protocol, and come as a simple tourist, but our able and kind new ambassador, Bill Mahoney of Phoenix, Arizona, persuaded me that this might appear to be an act of discourtesy. He therefore arranged for us to make a call of courtesy upon President Nkrumah.

This turned out to be a rich experience. Osagyefo was in rare form — radiant with that God-given quality of leadership which makes him a most exceptional person. He remembered Emily perfectly, and the conversation was just short of uproarious all of the time. When we were about to leave, he said to her, "Last time I gave him presents. This time he doesn't count, and they are all for you. I gave him books on birds, and now I give you one about fish" (which he autographed). Then he gave her a lovely "traditional urn" of a new type of native art work which is called *pore* in the Twi language. She loved it, but I had to carry it all the way home in a flight bag, wrapped up in dirty shirts.

But after we had left, there came most unexpectedly a reverse bit of drama of the sort which still makes Africa incomprehensible to Americans, and one which I kept strictly to myself until I had left Ghana.

As we drove away from Flagstaff House, we had an hour of free time ahead of us, so I decided to go west toward Takoradi for half an hour, and then come back.

We had just made the turn when we found our way barred by a police block which had been thrown across the road. Several cars besides ours were waiting their turn. The officers were entirely courteous, but they made us get out, and then not only searched our car for concealed weapons, but also make a token search of our persons, done by a policeman for me, and a police-woman for Emily. I could not help asking myself as I stood there on the highway watching the hood of our car being raised, and the seats being pulled out, where else in the world it could happen that two people could be cordially received by the chief of state, and then within an hour after leaving his presence be searched for weapons by his police. Yet I had to admit that it was not to be wondered at that Osagyefo was on his guard, for only a few days before a serious attempt had been made to assassinate him.

Such is my memory of Ghana and of Kwame Nkrumah. I can form no clear image as yet of the future of this exciting country, and I come back to the thought that this may have been true in 1776 as thoughtful Europeans speculated on what lay ahead for the United States. I would so like to know, and I hope that I still may be spared for a long enough period of years to make at least an intelligent guess as to how it will all come out.

15

❖ ❖

❖

Memories of the First World War

NO MAN of my age can turn back the pages of
memory without feeling a lump in his throat
as he comes to the year 1917–1918, for, whether he was
in uniform or not, the war completely transformed his
life.

My sequence was first Officers' Training Camp at
Fort Sheridan, Illinois; then training with troops in the
85th Infantry Division at Camp Custer, Michigan; then
overseas as aide to Brigadier General Thomas B. Dugan,
who commanded a brigade in the 85th.

Patsy Dugan, the men called him (emphasis on the
last syllable), and what a magnificent soldier he was!
He taught me the full meaning of the word duty, yet
he did so in a way that filled my heart with affection
for him, as well as profound respect. The time still
left for him in the military service was short, and he
knew it. Old cavalryman that he was, and veteran of
Indian campaigns, there was no chance that General

Pershing, who had once been a junior officer under his command, would advance him to any post of senior responsibility. Retirement was at hand, yet never for a moment did he falter in measuring up to the highest traditions of the United States Army. I learned from him habits of self-discipline, and precision accuracy in the carrying out of commitments which no other experience in my life could have given me.

I had many adventures while serving on his staff, the memories of which I cherish, and here are some of them.

❖ ❖ ❖

The first President of the United States that I ever saw in the flesh — and there was a great deal of it — was William Howard Taft. I was quite close to him — for a moment, that is. The truth is that I had the high privilege of holding his overcoat. And what a coat it was! It was an enormous coonskin job such as used to be seen in those days on the fifty-yard line at Harvard-Yale football games. I estimated its weight at fifty pounds, and felt confident that it could stand alone if placed in a corner.

Let me hastily add, however, that Mr. Taft was not the President of the United States at the time. Quite to the contrary. This was the winter of 1917–1918, and in 1912 he had received the worst beating of any presidential candidate in our entire history.

The locale of this bizarre encounter of mine was the stage of the large auditorium at Camp Custer, the training area for the 85th Division. Mr. Taft had been invited to come and address the soldiers, and the place was packed to the rafters. All of the military brass were on the platform, including my general, and since as a mere first lieutenant I was sitting in the back row, I was nearest at hand when our distinguished guest entered. Veteran that I was, having almost six months of military training behind me, I sprang instantly to attention, and helped him to remove his gigantic outer garment. Wise he was to have worn it, too, for the temperature outside was near zero. But what to do with it during the address was quite a problem. I finally laid it on three chairs, just offstage.

Never have I heard a public figure make a better speech to a soldier audience than Mr. Taft made that night. He took those homesick boys up into the mountaintop of inspiration, filling their hearts with intense patriotism and dedication to the task that lay ahead, yet deftly pausing from time to time to find an appropriate means of giving way to one of those infectious chuckles for which he was famous. We were poised between deep emotion and roaring laughter all evening.

His opening was unique. The major general who was then commanding our division was a bit heavy-handed in his introduction, and said in a ringing burst of oratory. "You go down to Washington and tell them that this division is ready, and wants to fight."

The suggestion that with only Utah and Vermont standing to his credit in the 1912 election, Mr. Taft should go down to Washington and tell anybody, least of all Mr. Wilson, what to do was a little too much, and with a hearty laugh that engulfed his entire countenance, he turned to the general and said, "Who did you say I should tell?"

When the address was finished, the cheering had stopped, and the time had come for me to hoist that enormous coat once more onto those capacious shoulders, I knew that I should never forget that evening, and the memory of it is still as vivid for me as though it had happened yesterday.

❖   ❖   ❖

I made my first airplane flight during the summer of 1918, and while the aviation industry was still pretty young. I have logged a lot of miles in the air since, but I have had no greater thrills, and probably faced no greater risks, than I did on that occasion.

My division, the 85th, left Camp Custer at Battle Creek early in July of 1918, but while we were awaiting the assembly of our fleet of ocean transports we were camped temporarily under canvas on Long Island. One day General Dugan took me with him for an inspection of the two adjoining air fields at Mineola, and I think that he was just as excited at what we saw as I was, for it was totally new to both of us.

We watched innumerable men go up, and were shown all kinds of ships, including Curtis training planes, Curtis Scouts, Italian and American Capronis, big bombers with Liberty motors, Havilands, French monoplanes, and many others. Everywhere we went I begged for a ride, but all of the officers told the same story —

that it was flatly forbidden. Finally I had a talk with the lieutenant who was in charge of the hangars, and he gave me the tip that maybe he could sneak me up in a plane that was being tested, the record on which would go no farther than his desk. He was as good as his word, and next day in the middle of the morning he pulled up outside my tent in his flivver, and called to me to jump in quick.

He ran me over to his field, had a single-motor, two-seater plane backed around, and introduced me to the sergeant who was to take me up. With deadpan face he said, "No stunts, sergeant! Just straight flying!" The sergeant saluted, said "Yes, sir," and we moved out.

Here is how I recorded the adventure in my war time journal:

Almost before I knew it I had been up for what they call "a little jazz around." I flew for over half an hour, and went up as high as 2500 feet. The sergeant wouldn't admit that he had done anything but straight flying, but from my point of view it had all the necessary tickle in it. There is no use in believing these golden-tongued liars who claim they never bat an eye on their first ride, for they know perfectly well that there are times when their backbone ruffles up like a cat's. For the first five minutes I felt very strange, and had to tell myself severely to stop wondering whether the sergeant was a good pilot. Then I got fairly nonchalant and enjoyed the big eyeful I got by looking down. The fields were like a doll's garden, and the distant ocean like a lazy play stream. But just as the beauty of it all came over me, the sergeant began to mix them up on me. He first gave me the great-grandfather of all rollercoaster thrills. He did this a few times (drawing of ocean waves). Then he straightened out for a ways, and suddenly winged up sideways on his right plane, and over to the opposite on his left plane, and back straight, all in one motion.

And when he shut her off, and let her hang there motionless for a minute (it seemed to me), and then nosed her over for a glide of a few hundred feet, my cowardly stomach just simply deserted me, and my one thought was what a fine big belt I had around me. However, money couldn't buy my satisfaction at having been up, and I stride among the other ordinary officers around here with a halo of wild-eyed envy surrounding me. The war is already a success as far as I am concerned.

❖   ❖   ❖

I once saw a Secretary of War in wartime. The man was Newton D. Baker, the time was late in 1918, and the place was an open field well behind the front lines in northeastern France, near the city of Langres. The Secretary was being driven along the main highway, obviously on his way to General Pershing's headquarters at Chaumont, and stopped when he saw American soldiers in uniform moving in open formation toward a small hill that lay ahead. Quite naturally he wondered what was going on.

Suddenly we saw him laugh good-naturedly, and settle down to watch. He had apparently just been told that we were student officers from the Army School of the Line, and that we were endeavoring to solve a problem of tactics under the stern eye of an instructor. Each of us was engaged in preparing suitable commands to give to Sergeant Hill, that mythical noncommissioned officer who turned up at all First World War training camps, in order that we might capture the imaginary German machine gun that was holding up our advance.

We were young, we were a long way from home, we were deeply frustrated at being in that field instead of in combat a few kilometers to the north, and that friendly smile from the man who was the symbol of the entire military power of our country gave our morale a tremendous lift.

❖ ❖ ❖

No living veteran of World War I can fail to have the most vivid and poignant memory of Armistice Day in 1918. On that solemn but exultant day it seemed incredible to those of us who were in France that this total war, which had so completely taken possession of our lives and to which each one of us had brought a feeling of personal dedication that was our supreme passion, had suddenly stopped. There had been rumors that this might happen, but we had given them no credence, and then suddenly came the end. What a tumult of emotions we had! Grief for our comrades from training-camp days who had made the ultimate sacrifice; infinite relief that the horror was finished; intense homesickness and longing for those at home, which for me included a baby daughter whom I had never seen; and sullen frustration that training must go on. On that historic day I was still fighting imaginary battles at the Army School of the Line in Langres, not far from the front, and here is how I recorded the explosive news in my journal.

What a day, and what a night! In the middle of the morning we knew that the Armistice had been signed and that hostilities would cease at eleven, and as we sat in the map room finishing the morning's terrain problem, we watched the minutes tick off, saying more than once that we hoped no one would be bumped off in the last hour, and then at eleven we hurriedly signed the papers and started the noise. After lunch, Col. Miller, the commandant, assembled us in the big room, and we knew what was coming, but a well-stimulated youth beat him to it, and while we were waiting, he delivered a pathetic address, begging us not to slack off in our work. After that the entire two hundred sang "Home Sweet Home" with more volume than I had ever heard put into it before. And when the Colonel did finally tell us the war would continue in Langres, if nowhere else, it was very funny.

The French were most peculiar about it. The Americans had the telegram first, and when we told them they wouldn't believe it, having been fooled no end of times before. Gradually they began to believe it, but still they were more or less in a daze, and all the afternoon we growled about their being phlegmatic. But about five the cathedral bells broke loose with a joyous roar, and the whole town caught it. Excited workmen mended the street lamps, such as they are, and tonight they are lighted for the first time in years. Flags of all the Allies hung from the houses, and red Japanese lanterns were dug up from no one knows where.

Tonight *tout le monde* is on the street. Men, women, boys — French or foreign, they surge round the streets howling. Americans buy champagne like soda water, and hot grog flows in bucketsful. When I came in just now at eight o'clock a chap with a Very pistol was firing signal rockets into the air above Diderot's statue that stands in the square, to the vast enjoyment of the cosmopolitan crowd around him. In short, the evening has reached the point where all the nonalcoholics go in and write letters. *Finie — la guerre,* the phrase which has been on every lip, will soon be a permanent part of the world's vocabulary.

16

✧   ✧
✧

Miniatures

IN ONE'S gallery of memories there are many full-sized portraits and panoramas, but there are also miniatures, sharp vignettes of people, places, or events which had no earthshaking significance when recorded but which nevertheless, and perhaps for that very reason, we value greatly.

Here are a few of the choicest from my own collection:

My sudden plunge into the torment of postwar Europe in 1948 as a member of the Marshall Plan team had an impact on my life far beyond what I was aware of at the time. Each day brought me new exposures to the thought streams of that turbulent period for which I was unprepared by either training or background, and I am sure that this was the experience of all Americans who were involved in that extraordinary undertaking.

For us the Europe of today, in which the ancient animosities have been moderated among the free nations,
is an incredible miracle of history. Frenchmen, Luxemburgers, Belgians and Hollanders now work daily within
the Common Market in cordial collaboration with their
colleagues from the other side of the Rhine, but in
1948 they were still dominated by an active hatred of
all Germans, mingled with fear which was so intense
that no page of mine can ever hope to recapture it.
From the first moment of my arrival in Paris I had to

As soon as Averell Harriman set me right that my
own.

As soon as Averell Harriman set me right that my
first job as his steel and coal consultant was to find
out, both for him and for myself, what my job really
was, I knew that the way to begin was to visit the industrial areas.

I traveled first to Metz, and my companions were
three key figures from the French steel industry who
had been recruited for the purpose by Jean Monnet's
office. Their interest in me was unbounded, for in their
eyes I was the symbol of an astonishing new phenomenon
which they did not clearly understand. The Marshall
Plan concept was still an enigma to them. They could
not guess what my purposes were, and I am sure that
they greatly overestimated my authority. I suspect that
at times they even thought that I had a blank check
in my briefcase.

We left Paris by train late one afternoon, and as the
twilight came on the countryside was lovely. It was

countryside, too, that was sacred to Americans — first Chateau Thierry, then the Argonne with Mont Sec on the skyline, and finally the Verdun area far off to the left. My companions had little English, and they followed a pattern that later became very familiar to me. As the conversation became serious they forgot their English, and we had to get ahead as best we could with my French. For three hours we tackled one by one the various great questions of the day, and then suddenly at one point, in an effort to introduce a lighter touch, they asked me what I did for a vacation. I was weary with conflicting emotions, and, welcoming the change, I described to them my island and summer cottage on Lake Michigamme up near Lake Superior. They asked me whether I ever encountered wild animals there, so I gave them a lurid tale of having seen a black bear with three cubs, a coyote, and many deer. This did not particularly advance the Marshall Plan, but it did give me relief from the strain that I was experiencing. Besides, it helped my French.

Next day we visited the Hagondange steel plant, where we were joined by more industrial leaders. They were possessed of the same insatiable curiosity about the Marshall Plan, and it was in talking with that group that I first came face to face with the fierce hatred felt for the Germans by the French. These men were haunted by the fear that under Allied controls the steel industry of the Ruhr might be permitted, and assisted, to develop faster than was possible in Lorraine, and they were openly suspicious of every move that the United States was making. They suspected an evil purpose in everything that was being done.

They needed coke for their blast furnaces badly, and they righteously declared that their needs should be fully met before any tonnage whatsoever should be allocated to the Ruhr, which was where it was being produced. When I asked them whether Lorraine would ship any of its iron ore to the Ruhr, in exchange for badly needed dollars, they said that their men would strike before they would let that happen. When I said that I doubted whether Germany could get enough ore from Sweden to supply its plants, and asked where else the Ruhr could get it if the output from Lorraine was cut off, they merely shrugged their shoulders. Their formula for Marshall Plan aid was simple: it should be divided in proportion to suffering, and France should receive the greater share because it had had the greatest suffering. Seen against this background, what a marvel it is that these ancient enemies are now united in a joint effort to promote the welfare of Europe as a whole.

Happily, there was also a brighter side to my visit. These same gentlemen overwhelmed me with traditional French hospitality. By showing personal kindness to me they endeavored to express their deep appreciation for a generosity which they realized had no precedent in history, and they did this in spite of the fact that they did not as yet fully comprehend either its extent or its objectives.

The medium chosen for this hospitality was a ceremonial luncheon which they gave for me. It lasted three hours and was again the sort of ordeal for which I was quite unprepared. We began with hors d'oeuvres. Then came fish, after which we had lamb chops, then beef, and after that cheese, and finally cherries and peaches. For beverages we began with Mirabelle, the famous native aperitif, which we consumed while standing. At table, with the fish we had Riesling, the local white wine. With the lamb chops we were served Médoc, and with the roast beef a red Burgundy. With the dessert they gave us a horrible native liqueur which tasted to me like distilled lightning, and with the coffee this was repeated demi-demi with Martel brandy.

Then back to the steel plant. By that time I was speaking French one hundred words to the minute.

Such were the sacrifices that a man was called upon to make for his country while helping to bring the Marshall Plan to Europe.

In a French hotel the best possible person to know is the gouvernante, or head housekeeper. Should she smile on you in the presence of the staff, you will have more bath towels immediately, and should she at the same time call you by name, and stop to chat with you in the corridor, innumerable blessings will follow, such as greater alacrity in the removal of the breakfast table.

The delightful lady who bore this responsibility at the Crillon Hotel in my Marshall Plan days entered my life rather dramatically, and the benevolence which followed was a great asset to me in those soapless days.

One afternoon just after lunch, when I was alone in my small suite, there came a knock on my door, and when I opened it there this lady stood. Hesitantly she asked if she might come in, and when I assured her that she would be most welcome she crossed to the large chair, sat down, and in a rapid flow of excited French opened her heart to me. She said that the pride and passion of her life was her autograph book, that she had heard that I was a friend of Paul Hoffman, and she wondered whether she might dare to hope that I would be willing to ask him to add lustre to its pages by giving her his autograph.

Paul had the largest suite in the hotel (which he paid for himself), and it was on the floor immediately above mine.

My capacity for subversive action having been aroused by her inquiry and the initiative which she had displayed in furthering her project, and sensing what her friendship could mean to me in those times of general shortages, I asked her to go and get her book and let me look at it. She was almost afraid to be encouraged, but her face brightened with anticipation, and she rushed out.

In no time at all she was back, and when I opened her handsome book I found that it did in fact contain a distinguished group of autographs. The latest was that of the Shah of Persia, who had been the previous occupant of Paul's suite.

I asked her whether she had her pass key with her,

and when she replied that she did, I beckoned to her to follow me. Up the stairs we went, and when I tapped on Paul's door, and there was no answer, I told her to open it with her key. Here her nerve all but failed her. She was aghast, for this was most irregular. To permit another person to enter the great man's suite when he was not there was just one step short of sacrilege, but I insisted, and in we went.

I opened the book so as to display the half-empty page just below the signature of the Shah, and laid it out on a table. Across the face of it I laid a note which said, "Paul: If you love me, sign your name and ask no questions. Clarence." Then I led the terrified lady out. She was quivering with excitement and apprehension.

The next day when I came back to my room for a moment in the late morning, I found the door open. Inside was the gouvernante, radiant with satisfaction, supervising the activities of two workmen.

They were perched on stepladders, and were engaged in hanging over my divan a perfectly gorgeous, and valuable, old French painting.

She had spent the preceding afternoon covertly watching Paul's suite, had seen him come and go, had dared to go in a second time, and there she had found his handsome autograph meticulously done immediately below that of the Shah.

The friendship which I thus formed has never faltered through the years. It still brings me blessings.

❖   ❖   ❖

When two men discuss a business transaction over a luncheon table they are engaging in a custom that is both ancient and honorable. It can be profitable too — provided that all goes well. I tried it once, however, under circumstances that became so ludicrous that I have forgotten everything about the luncheon except how it ended.

A man called me up one morning and asked me if I could meet him for lunch to discuss what he said was a very urgent matter. I had not known him well, and he gave me no clue as to what the subject was. I demurred at first on the ground that my schedule for that day was unusually complex, but he insisted that he would suit his convenience to mine. So I yielded, and said that I could fit it in if I did not have to go far from my office.

"Fine," he answered. "How would the Union League Club do?"

"O.K.," I said, for that was only two blocks from my office. "Make it at twelve-thirty sharp, if you can."

When I walked into the Club he was standing just inside the front door, and, after checking my hat hurriedly, I stepped into the elevator with him. He plunged immediately into his subject, and was so preoccupied with it that he gave no thought to which was the right floor for the dining room. Not being a member of the Union League Club myself, I had forgotten what floor it was on, but I got off when the rest of the men did, and led him along. He was still talking.

We were shown to a good table, but we hardly noticed

where it was, for we were doing business all of the time, and we ordered our luncheons almost automatically.

At the end of an hour I had to leave. We both looked around at the same time, and the waiter promptly brought the check, laying it down between us. I did not pick it up because I was not a member, and my friend just kept on talking.

I grew embarrassed, and must have betrayed that by my manner, for he suddenly stopped in the middle of a sentence, and a look of horror came over his face. Then he stammered out, "Aren't you a member here?" Nonplussed, all I could say was "No! Aren't you?" "Oh Lord, no," he answered, "I thought you were." That triggered it, and together we both burst into such hilarious laughter that everyone around us turned and looked at our table.

So the waiter had to get the headwaiter, and the headwaiter had to get the manager, and after much maneuvering a way was found by which I might pay the check in cash, after which we sneaked out of the Club much wiser than when we came in.

What the deal was about, or what happened to it, I do not seem to remember.

Pity the man who tries to write a book without a secretary, and pity especially the individual who dares to embark upon that mad pursuit without as devoted and effective a secretary as mine. Her name is Miss

Naomi Bradley, and she and I have been a team for
more years than either of us would care to reveal. In
fact, hers has been almost a life sentence, and during
all of that time she has borne with my derelictions,
suffered under my impatience, and struggled against
heavy odds to make me look smart. Above all, she has
resisted what must be for her a great temptation, that
of writing a book herself — about her boss — in which
she would tell the truth, the whole truth, and nothing
but the truth. I am satisfied, however, that she is much
too kind ever to do that.

That I have made utterly unreasonable demands
upon her loyalty is undoubtedly the subject of common
talk among her friends. For example, there is literally
no hour of the day during which I have not given her
dictation. When strikes have been on, I have kept her
at her desk straight through the night. As for travel,
there is no means of transportation, except perhaps a
helicopter, in which we have not carried on our work.
Trains, planes, boats, automobiles, we have done them
all.

Twice she flew to Europe with me in the course of
government missions in which I participated. (Always
at my expense, please note.) I can still see her on a certain evening in London. We had worked hard all day,
and then I had to go off for a dinner at a London club.
One of my friends in the British steel industry called
for me at Claridge's, and as we started to leave the hotel
he turned to me, and said, "I am thinking about that
remarkable secretary of yours. She is having no fun at

all over here; just works all the time. Give her a ring on the phone, tell her that we are coming back to pick her up at ten o'clock, and that we are going to take her to the Savoy for the supper show." So I did just that, being a little ashamed not to have thought of it myself.

When we came back later, as planned, I beheld the picture that has always lingered in my mind as the acme of secretarial devotion. There she was, seated at the desk in my suite, smartly dressed in an evening gown, but still pounding her typewriter. The job which she had begun was not done, and she could not bear to see the time wasted.

Our most ludicrous adventure, however, is a vignette from Arizona. During the latter part of February one year, Emily and I had gone out as usual to be with friends at our favorite vacation spot, which is Kenyon Ranch, at Tubac, just north of the Mexican border. I was still active in business, and made it a point to keep in touch with what was going on in my office by telephoning Miss Bradley twice a week. On one particular morning she reported trouble. A crisis had arisen which needed my attention at once, and not wanting to interrupt our vacation, I asked her to get on a plane promptly and bring the whole file out to me. By the next evening she had arrived at the ranch, and my greeting to her went like this: "Make yourself at home around here as best you can tomorrow morning, for I am going to ride at ten o'clock, and we will take this up right after lunch."

But I had reckoned without the ranch practical jokers, a group in which normally I enjoyed full membership. There were three of us who were usually at the bottom of whatever deviltry went on: the late Morton Bailey, advertising manager of the *Saturday Evening Post,* Dr. Cy Sturgis, the distinguished chief medical officer of the clinics at the University of Michigan, and myself. The sudden arrival of Miss Bradley was too much for these fellow comedians of mine, and they later confessed to me that their conversation had gone like this: "Oh, ho! Big shot, eh? Has to have his secretary come out — no less! We'll fix him!" And fix me they did.

Next morning when it came time to ride, I went pounding down the path to the corral in my dude outfit, and what did I find? There, seated on a horse and laughing at me, was my Miss Bradley, togged out in levis, flannel shirt and boots, which they had borrowed for her. The reins were loose on the horse's neck, and in her two hands she held her notebook and pencil.

Nothing would then do but that I must mount up, pull my horse alongside of hers, and go through with the act of dictating to her from the saddle, while she scribbled notes. Cameras snapped on every side, but Cy Sturgis took the best photograph, which he mailed directly to Miss Bradley, obviously not trusting me.

The picture was a sensation at home, and when it appeared over my secretary's desk the sentiment of the other ladies was expressed this way by one of them: "We are not surprised at this at all. The only thing which Mr. Randall hasn't yet asked Naomi to do is to take dictation underwater, and we expect that any time now."

17

✧ ✧
✧

Not People, but Places

THE HIGH spots in life can be places as well as people.

The Acropolis, the Colosseum, the Roman Forum, the Chapel of St. Francis of Assisi, Notre Dame at Paris, the Mona Lisa, the Cathedral at Chartres, all bring home to the traveler a sense of the depth of history from which our civilization has sprung. Conversely, the Communist wall of East Berlin brings home a doubt as to whether that civilization can long survive.

Then there are the great miracles of the world, such as the Taj Mahal, which is so breathtaking in its beauty that you are led to wonder whether ours is after all the greatest civilization the world has ever seen.

What could be more picturesque than Fujiyama lifting its crest through the clouds over Japan, or what more stirring for the imagination than the temples of Bangkok?

The truly great thrill in travel, however, is suddenly to come upon something which becomes yours by right of discovery, something which you have never even heard of before, something which no neighbor of yours has ever photographed.

It was that way one day with Emily and me when we were walking alone among the ruins of ancient Carthage. We came to the tiny port where Hannibal must have embarked his elephants, and there was a little boy playing on the shore. He was digging in the sand with a shovel, as little boys do. Suddenly he ran screaming to his mother, holding something in his hand. He had found an old Punic coin which had been lying buried there for centuries.

Then there was Sabratha, the ruined Roman city which lies a few miles outside the city of Tripoli in Libya, and which dates from the sixth century B.C. Here the gleaming white columns have for their background the blue of the Mediterranean: a photographer's paradise with not a postcard vendor in sight. We had not even known that it existed until we saw it.

There was the day in Kano, Nigeria, when suddenly, without advance planning, we came upon the Moslem mosque, probably the finest public structure to be found anywhere south of the Sahara. It was a holy day, and we saw ten thousand followers of Islam approach for worship, pausing along the highway to buy a jug of water with which to perform their ritual ablutions.

And what could be more thrilling than to fly as we did through the Himalayas, and across Nepal, with the mountains of Tibet, land of mystery, on the left, and the snow-capped peak of Everest dead ahead?

Latest in our series of discoveries, however, and in some respects the most thrilling, were the two dramatic countries of Basutoland and Swaziland, which lie in the very southernmost part of the continent of Africa. I use the word countries advisedly, for though geographically they are within the land mass over which the Republic of South Africa exercises sovereignty in general, they are political enclaves that are not subject to that sovereignty. They are governed by Her Majesty the Queen of Great Britain, Basutoland as a crown colony, and Swaziland as a protectorate. Soon to receive their independence, these little-known principalities might conceivably be the medium through which a new pattern will be formed for the ultimate cooperative relationship between whites and blacks throughout the continent.

We flew first to Basutoland, circling the capital city of Maseru, and the rugged promontories that surround it, before landing on a good grass strip in front of an air terminal which was the smallest we had ever seen but one of the most attractive. There was no commercial air service yet, but we had an excellent two-motor chartered plane.

The scenery in Basutoland is rugged beyond description. Always on the skyline are rock formations of unusual shapes and colors which are so like Arizona that anyone who loves our own Southwest will be enraptured. Rising above Maseru in the immediate foreground is a mountain that is cut through at the summit by a deep gorge called Lancers Pass, where the British fought a fierce battle with a recalcitrant chief in the nineteenth century.

As explorers we had one lucky break when we set out into the country from Maseru. A car had been sent over for our use from South Africa, but the driver did not know the area well, and on our very first morning he got lost. We thus wound up by accident in a remote mountain district where life was primitive indeed, though the road was not bad at all. Afterwards we found that we had been well on the way toward Thaba Putsua, the traditional burial place of Basuto chiefs.

Late in the afternoon we drove out to Roma to see the only university in any of the three protectorates. It had 170 students, of whom 29 were women. Built and carried on by the Oblate Fathers, it is a great credit to the Roman Catholic Chuch, and has had a profound influence for good in this tiny country. The territory now has over 90 per cent literacy, which is said to be the highest in all of black Africa.

Flying out again was another thrill. First of all, at takeoff, our pilot faced an unusual hazard. It was Sunday morning, and a group of enterprising young Africans were using the grass landing strip as a golf course, but we threaded our way through them successfully.

We took off across the Caledon River, which marks the boundary with the Orange Free State of South Africa, and below us was a magnificent panorama. There were deep gorges, high craggy outcrops rising from the plain, and a majestic mountain range ahead. Gradually the rough terrain yielded to cultivation, and we passed over large estates developed by the thrifty Boers, with the mansion house in the center, surrounded by trees, and the cottages for the Bantu workers some distance away.

And let no one think that we suffered any privations while in Basutoland. Those Americans who have no image of Africa other than lions and Pygmies seem to think that all travelers who go there organize a safari and sleep in tents. They should see the Lancers Inn at Maseru, which is not only modern and adequate but delightful.

Next came Swaziland, and a stay at the Highland View Hotel in the capital city of Mbabane, where again the accommodations and service were all that the most demanding tourist could ask for.

How exciting that first evening was! Never before in our lives, not even when we were in Nepal, had we felt so remote from our familiar scenes, yet it was all beautiful and impressive. Before going in to a delicious dinner we sat for awhile out on the veranda of the hotel, and there in the darkness of the sky the Southern Cross was shining. Even to our unpracticed eyes it was unmistakable; three stars at the top to mark the summit and the arms of the cross, and then two below to outline the supporting column. We were entranced. Next morning we found that the daytime view was still more breathtaking — fifty miles to the horizon across hills and plains, a sight so unforgettable that it is rightly called Ezulwini, or Heavenly Valley.

Spanning Swaziland from west to east, or from Mbabane to Stegi, is a fine highway, much of it hard surface, which is a joy to the traveler, not only for his peace of mind as to comfort and safety, but for what he will see. There will be tick birds in a tree, children dancing and playing outside their rondavels, a crazy mixture of cattle, sheep, goats, and little boys moving out of a pasture and down toward a water hole, a woman doing her washing in a stream, the headman of a village in his colorful robes, and with luck a lady witch doctor.

But it is the modern and not the primitive which astounds the visitor to this remote area today.

Swaziland is humming with activity. Endowed with remarkable natural resources, it is on the march, and the time is rapidly approaching when it can stand on its own feet economically. In the northwest, for example, there is an important asbestos mine and a vast new iron ore project. Running down the western boundary from Pigg's Peak to Usutu is a vast man-made forest that stretches as far as the eye can see. Then there are citrus and avocado groves, pineapple plantations, broad fields of sugar and of maize, and a healthy agriculture in general. The Swazis sense their oncoming prosperity, know that they need the partnership of the white man, and are determined to create a political atmosphere in which he will feel comfortable.

Sometimes, however, their urge to be modern brings

a smile to the traveler's face. On the main street in Mbabane there is a single traffic light, only they don't call it that either there or in South Africa. The word is robot. The story is this. When King Sobhuza visited London he saw traffic lights for the first time, and decided that as a matter of prestige his country must have one. It is pain to all concerned, for there is not yet traffic enough to regulate, and besides, the horses do not seem to understand it.

It is our firm opinion that no one who visits either Basutoland or Swaziland can fail to want to go back, and that when American tourists eventually discover these exciting new countries they will go there in droves.

18

✧ ✧
✧

Commencement Chaos

A COLLEGE commencement is America to me. No experience in life can bring home to a man more vividly the infinite capacity of the American people for continuing self-development than to be the commencement speaker, and look at those upturned faces. Best of all is the privilege of doing this out of doors on a shaded campus.

The parents are there, surrounded by other members of the family, beaming with pride and happiness that their hopes and sacrifices have been fulfilled and that a long-cherished goal has been attained.

The faculty are there, in cap and gown, sensing deeply once more both the satisfactions and the responsibilities that are theirs as they devote their lives to the guidance of the oncoming generation.

And down in front are the graduating class themselves, sitting rather nervously on the edges of their chairs. In every eye you can see a surge of mixed emotions; on the one hand an exultant gleam of "Well, I made it!" and on the other apprehension over what lies ahead.

Behind the speaker are the Board of Trustees, who are deeply moved by the drama which they are witnessing, and who will leave the ceremony more determined than ever to make this the very best institution of its kind in the country.

It is little wonder that some of the most inspiring and significant pronouncements in our history have found expression on such occasions.

The one that I can never forget, for example, was the address given at the Harvard Commencement in June of 1947 by General George C. Marshall, then Secretary of State, in which he announced the Marshall Plan. Seldom, if ever, before has a greater impact been made upon the welfare of the world by words spoken in public than during those few moments when that distinguished American stood before his Harvard audience.

The contingencies of life being what they are, however, the sublime is forever under constant threat from the ridiculous. The grotesque can intrude within even the august serenity of a college commencement, and I hope no one will think me irreverent if with sinful glee I record a few such seismic disturbances which I have witnessed.

There was the time at Dartmouth, for example, when a dog took over the conduct of the exercises. As is customary on that magnificent campus, the ceremonies were being held out of doors. The day was beautiful, and the sky cloudless. An unusually large crowd was present, and as the pageantry got under way we were all waiting in eager anticipation. I was on the platform, and my wife was in the second row.

The salutatorian, who was a most attractive young man, had just begun his address when down the aisle raced a large collie dog. What caused this angry canine intruder to resent so bitterly what was going on about him was never made clear, but he was definitely most unhappy about the whole proceeding. Down in front a man was standing up, and sound was coming from that direction, so he promptly decided that there was the place from which he could deliver his protest. Taking his stance directly in front of the podium, he voiced his lament in a series of strident howls, and they were so powerful that he froze the salutatory address right in the middle of a sentence. The poor young man had absolutely no choice but to stop.

Consternation swept the audience. No one dared to laugh. No one dared to move. Then suddenly came the action. In from both sides rushed a corps of green-clad ushers, "members of the Green Key," and the dog began to run. He was not fast enough off the mark, however, and he never had a chance. One stalwart usher, who should have been awarded his varsity letter forthwith, made a flying tackle that was right on target. He fell on the miscreant, pinned him down until help arrived, and then carried him off into the outer regions.

When quiet had been restored, the brave salutatorian

had to resume once more his effort to take the great audience up onto the heights of inspiration. And I must say that he did it with admirable poise and self-discipline.

Once at Brown University it was Dr. Henry Wriston himself who brought down the house. He was nothing if not forthright and decisive. The exercises were drawing to a close, and the time had come for the awarding of the degrees. The line of seniors formed and began its march up the steps to the stage, moving two by two. It was obvious that this would be a fairly long undertaking, for there were several hundred of them.

Dr. Wriston rose from where he was sitting in the center of the stage and, by way of preparing to receive them, crossed to a series of tables which had been so arranged as to give him ready access to the diplomas when they would be handed to him one by one. It soon became clear, however, that this part of the ceremony had not been rehearsed, and that something was radically wrong. After fewer than a dozen of the class had been presented to the president, he suddenly raised his hand in an authoritative gesture that stopped everything.

The object of his displeasure was obvious. He was most unhappy at the way in which these tables had been arranged. The motions that he was compelled to make in handing out the diplomas were clumsy, and the orderly progress of the column of seniors was impeded. So, spurning all help, he attacked the problem himself, and personally moved the tables into a new pattern of arrangement which better suited his purposes. This accomplished, he gave the signal to resume, and the awarding of the diplomas went happily forward again.

I made up my mind right then and there that the business world had lost a great executive when the community of scholars claimed Dr. Wriston for its own.

At Harvard my moment of commencement mirth was private, but equally convulsing. I was sitting in the front row on the platform, trying desperately to look important. My companion on my right, who was about to receive an honorary degree, was a delightful gentleman about whom I had heard much, and all of it good, but whom I had never met before.

Looking down at the audience, he observed a line of ladies seated in the second row, and asked if I knew who they were. I replied that they were the wives of those involved in the ceremonies, and that mine was the second from the aisle. All this in whispers. Then I added, "Isn't your wife there, too?" "My wife there?" he replied with loving laughter in his eyes, "Don't be ridiculous! She would not only not be on time, but she has probably gone to the wrong commencement."

Looking at these occasions as a distinctive category in the American scene, I am impressed with their diversity. Take the actual awarding of the honorary degree, for example. No two institutions do this in the same manner. It is as though the entire concept of academic freedom must be thus exemplified, for there is no universally accepted practice as to either words or action.

[158]

And of all presidents of colleges or universities whom I have been privileged to know, none was more unique in his emphasis upon the individuality of his customs than my good friend the late Dr. Gordon Chalmers of Kenyon College. In his practice, the degree recipient was required to kneel while the hood was being placed around his neck, and then to rise when the president intoned in Latin, *"Surge, Doctor!"* But this was not all. To make certain that there should be no untoward incident to mar the actual carrying out of the ceremony, he insisted upon a rehearsal, and this had to be done on the afternoon before the commencement.

When it came to be my turn to perform the rite in rehearsal, Dr. Chalmers was highly critical of me because I had knelt so far away from him that he could hardly reach me with the hood. This is how he admonished me. "Say, listen! Tomorrow be sure you get closer to me when you kneel, will you? This thing is no lasso, you know!" My great problem on the morrow, therefore, was this: instead of being overwhelmed with humility at the great honor which President Chalmers was bestowing on me as I knelt before him (as, of course, deep down in my heart I was), I had to struggle hard to keep my face straight. I kept thinking about that lasso all the time that my distinguished friend was carrying out the investiture.

I fear that this is the way it is with these august academic occasions. Those who make commencement addresses must face the stark reality that it may not be their words of wisdom but rather bizarre happenings such as these which will linger longest in the memories of those present.

19

❖ ❖
❖

The Lessons of Humiliation

WHEN THE TIME comes for a man to take the long backward look at his life, he cannot help but wonder which were the experiences which had the most important impact upon the development of his character.

Success is a powerful stimulant which leads to still greater endeavor, but when savored to the point of over-indulgence it leads to the disaster of overconfidence. The only safe antidote is genuine and continuing humility.

Failure is a caustic corrective, and it too is dangerous, for it can become such a severe depressant that it suspends effort. There is, moreover, the further difficulty that the dividing line between success and failure is often not immediately apparent. For example, there was a time in my life when it was my responsibility to acquire iron-mining prospects for my company. Some of my guesses have turned out well, but there are others which have not. They are lying idle, and the capital invested in them has not yet been recovered.

But as I see life now, the human experience which most deeply sears a man's soul, leaving a scar which never can be eliminated, is humiliation. There is no other therapy in the development of a man's character as powerful as the sudden realization that his conduct is considered unworthy by those about him.

I have had such periods of trauma, beginning with my boyhood.

The family life which I was privileged to share when growing up in Newark Valley was not marked by anger or violence. I was never spanked by my mother nor cuffed by my father; never taken to the woodshed. In fact, the only corporal punishment which I can remember receiving was six slaps on my right hand with a ruler from the principal of our school. I have no recollection as to what the offense was — whispering in class, I suspect — but I do recall my mother's reaction when I rushed home to tell her about it, which, by the way, was typical of our relationship. She made it clear to me that I had done wrong, putting it to me as a matter of conscience, but she was deeply disturbed at what the principal had done.

The most severe chastisement which I could receive was when she laid her hand upon my shoulder, looked into my face with those gentle eyes of hers, and said quietly, "Clarence, I am so disappointed! I had trusted you."

I remember vividly one such occasion.

It was late May, and my gang began to talk about going out again to the old swimming hole, which lay up the creek about a half mile from town. To reach it we had to cross an oat field which belonged to a farmer who must have understood boys, for he never complained to our parents about the zigzag path which we tramped across his freshly planted crop. One day after school one of the older youngsters called out, "Come on, let's go!" When I said that I would ask my mother, my remark was greeted with howls of derision. "Don't be silly," they jeered, "she won't ever find out." So I went.

But when I came home to supper, trying to appear innocent, Mother took one look at me, and said in an injured tone, "Clarence, your hair is wet! You have been swimming! Why would you do that without asking me first?" There was no threat, no anger, no reaching for the paddle. Just that look. The result was that I never did that again.

Then there was the time when I punched my sister Mabel. She was three years older than I, and gradually there built up inside me the animosity that adolescent lads sometimes develop toward an elder feminine member of the family who reaches maturity before they do. I stood it as long as I could, and then one day when we were walking up Main Street together she said something that triggered me, and I let her have it. It was a good solid poke right in the stomach, and she doubled up instantly. Unhappily, however, I had not looked behind me. I had hardly time to guffaw in glee at her discomfiture when I was lifted off my feet by an arm that was thrown round my neck. Following us by not

[163]

more than a half dozen steps was a tall powerful man, a friend of my father's. He shook me like a dirty rat, and when he had set me down again he roared in a voice that brought the neighbors to their windows, "Clarence Randall, as long as you live, don't you ever dare strike a woman again!" And I never have, — though there is still a little time left in my life.

In college I attracted no attention. I suffered from a severe inferiority complex. Conscious of the fact that I had come from west of the tracks, I considered it a privilege if any of the boys from Exeter or Groton as much as spoke to me.

When I reached Harvard Law School this changed. I stood high in my class scholastically, and this circumstance went promptly to my head. I suddenly decided that I had arrived, and grew cocky.

My contemporaries, however, promptly cut me down to size in most salutary fashion.

I was elected to the board of the Harvard Law Review, which was a coveted distinction, but to my inner discomfiture I was not chosen for one of the senior posts.

I entered the Ames Competition, which was training in advocacy through a series of moot cases, and survived through the early rounds, but was defeated in the finals, with the whole school looking on.

In the spring of senior year, I was nominated for the office of first marshall of my class, but here again I failed. I was soundly beaten, and deservedly, by that extraordinary scholar and fine citizen Bob Patterson, who went on to be Secretary of War during the last war.

It was not surprising, therefore, that when I withdrew to the wilds of Lake Superior to begin the practice of law in Ishpeming, Michigan, my classmates, who could not remember how to spell that word anyway, promptly drew a line through my name in their class directories and forgot me.

When later I left the North and came to Chicago to go to work in the steel industry, I suddenly realized that I was a very green novice among old hands, and my eager efforts to overcome that handicap brought me a very hilarious experience.

Since my first responsibilities had to do with iron ore, I decided that it was very important that I should get to know the top brass in the mining industry in Minnesota, and when late one October a group of these senior officers unexpectedly did me the honor of inviting me to go duck hunting with them, I leapt at the opportunity. Unearthing an old Parker shotgun which had belonged to Emily's grandfather, I jumped in a car and drove up to Nett Lake, which adjoined an Indian reservation in a very wild area toward the Canadian border.

I arrived just as the brethren were starting the afternoon hunt. A line of canoes had been pulled up on shore. Genuine birchbark they were, too. The technique was for each man to sit in the bow of a canoe with an Indian in the stern, and be paddled out through the wild rice beds, taking wing shots as the ducks jumped into the air.

It was here that my first chagrin began. By the time

they came to me in assigning canoes they had run out of Indian bucks, so they gave me a squaw. Now I happen to like Indians, and it wasn't her race that bothered me, but her sex. To be alone in a canoe from noon until dark, with an overly fat lady in the stern doing all the work, and this on a part of the lake where there was not another soul in sight, was definitely something new for me. Furthermore, I was obviously the only one to whom this had happened, and as we set out I could see that some of my colleagues were laughing so hard that they nearly fell out of their canoes.

To make it worse, we were the last ones back when night came. I had assumed that the squaw would tell me when it was time to return, while she took it for granted that I would tell her, so it was well after dark when I finally stepped ashore again.

I had shot one duck, and I was both cold and frustrated when I walked up the path toward the shack where we were to bed down. Nevertheless. I was true to my military training, and kept the shotgun pointed down.

When I entered the room, a poker game was in progress under the hanging kerosene lamp, and I was greeted with a medley of cheers and jeers as, with my duck in one hand and my gun in the other, I started to walk toward the fire, but stopped a moment to look over the shoulder of one of the players and see what he was holding.

That was when fate overtook me. What with the cold, and the squaw, and everything, I had forgotten to take the shells out of my gun, and as I turned to move on, I accidentally touched the triggers, and put two barrels of number five shot right through the cabin floor.

Needless to say, this did little to advance the prestige of the new assistant to the vice president of the Inland Steel Company.

It was in my mature years, however, that the supreme moment of anguish came into my life, just as I reached the climax of my active years in business.

One April afternoon, at the annual meeting of my company, I was elected president. I had reached my lifetime goal and went home that evening intoxicated with a high sense of achievement.

The dream was rudely shattered, however, on the following morning. One of the elder statesmen in our group, a man who possessed great influence on our Board of Directors, sent for me. When I had taken my seat across the desk from him, he said quietly, but firmly, "Clarence, I think you ought to know that I was strongly opposed to your becoming president of our company. I did not think that you were worthy of it."

I was stunned. Never in my life have I felt more hurt than when I walked soberly back to my desk to face a pile of congratulatory telegrams. For hours I was dumb with dismay. But the more I reflected upon the matter the more I realized that there was stark truth in many of the things he had said to me, and I resolved then and there to overcome the faults which he had listed for me with such candor.

The sequel was a happy one. That interview was the

beginning of a new friendship, one which deepened with the years and one which I came to value deeply.

It seems clear to me, therefore, that while success stimulates and failure brings dismay, the best therapy of all in the building of a man's character is an occasional heavy dose of humiliation.

20

❖ ❖
❖

Last Chapter

EVERY BOOK must have a last chapter. So must every great experience.

I have come to the end of a colorful adventure many times in my life, particularly during my retirement years, but never have I encountered a finale quite so dramatic as that which closed my service at the White House. It would be hard to imagine anything more utterly incongruous than that last afternoon and evening which terminated the administration of President Eisenhower and ushered in that of President Kennedy.

Those of us who were leaving White House assignments understood full well that never again would a privilege come to us as deeply gratifying as that which had been ours for the brief years during which we had served on the President's staff. We sensed also the difficult personal adjustments that lay immediately ahead for us when we would be compelled to put all this behind us and return to civilian life. Our emotions lay very close to the surface. Each time that we passed a colleague in the corridor of the Executive Office Building we realized that there went a man whom we should probably never in our lives see again, and a brooding sense of "This is the end" lay over all of our activities.

As we lunched together that day in the White House mess for the last time, we did not trust ourselves to talk about what was in our hearts, and we endeavored to keep the conversation light. For example, Gene Lyons, who was then the President's personnel advisor, told me that he thought it was important for me to know that if I were not offered a post by the new administration I would be entitled to unemployment compensation at the rate of $26.00 per week for twenty-six weeks.

Sitting down at my desk for the last time, with many urgent things still waiting to be done, I found it hard not to let myself become the captive of the ideas that were swirling in my mind.

Foremost was the thought that it was incredible, and altogether providential, that the President had been spared to fulfill his term, and by that I did not have in mind merely the ghastly personal risks which beset every man who becomes our chief executive. It was all that but more. Here was man who was six months older than I, the oldest President ever to hold that high office, who during his term had suffered a coronary thrombosis, a cerebral hemorrhage and a severe abdominal operation, but who nevertheless had never for a moment lost his courage. Still widely loved and respected, he had finished strong in every way.

On that last afternoon the minutes simply melted away. McGeorge Bundy had been designated as the officer of the incoming administration to whom I would transfer my responsibilities, and with whom I would carry out what was called the "transition." He came over to my office shortly after lunch and listened attentively to my explanation of what my function had been with respect to the coordination of foreign economic policy. I was strongly drawn to him with affection, for I sensed that I probably saw more clearly than he could at the time the heavy responsibilities that lay ahead for him.

Finally five o'clock came, marking the theoretical end of my government service, but when the actual moment arrived for closing my desk for the last time a denouement developed that was totally unexpected. Instead of being solemn, the end was ludicrous beyond belief.

I suddenly found that the question was not whether I should leave at five, but whether I could leave at all.

Nature had intervened, and I was marooned. A heavy snowstorm had begun to hit Washington about an hour before and was proving to be so utterly devastating in its impact that the whole city was rapidly becoming paralyzed.

Government offices had been let out early, and people everywhere were struggling to start their cars and get going, but hardly a wheel was turning. I could see the traffic from my window, and it barely crawled. To go out on the corner and stand there hoping to find a cab that would take me back to my hotel would be foolhardy indeed, particularly in view of my heart problem, so I asked my government secretary, Miss Margaret Quill, to telephone the White House garage and ask whether by any miracle they could let us have a car. The answer was negative. The officer in charge replied that there was just not a chance.

This brought us up short, so we decided to check our food reserves to see how long a siege we could take. We found that we had one box of triscuits and two bars of dietetic chocolate.

One by one the members of my staff closed their desks, shook my hand for the last time, and disappeared into the night, each to pursue some desperate experiment to get home. I had no choice but to stick it out, for I dared not try to walk.

Miss Quill and Dick Storch, the able attractive junior member of my staff, stood by. Being a bachelor, with no home duties to worry him, Dick boldly set out to organize a rescue expedition. About an hour later he telephoned that he had succeeded in walking to Georgetown, that the cars had been bumper to bumper all the way, that there was almost no movement at all, and that he was completely helpless to move his car because he had no chains. Cheerfully, however, he announced that he had formed a new plan, and that he would call us again as soon as he could. And call he did, but with great distress of mind. He had routed out a friend who did have chains for his car, and they had set forth bravely into the storm to rescue the boss, but they had undertaken the impossible. A half hour later they were hopelessly blocked by the stalled traffic. All that was left for Dick was to get to a telephone and report sorrowfully that he had no alternative but to terminate his service with me by leaving me to my fate.

This seemed to be the end, and Miss Quill and I began to reconcile ourselves to the thought that we would have to spend the entire night right there in our offices. Devoted secretary that she was, she simply turned calmly back to her desk, and continued tearing up my personal files. For me there was nothing left to do but lie down on my couch and stare at the ceiling.

Then, suddenly I had an inspiration. Happily, I remembered that there had been a bulletin put out that morning which said that the White House mess would be open that evening for dinner, so gaily I invited my secretary to dine with me, and we set forth. Getting there, however, took some doing. First of all, the elevator in our part of the building was not running, and we had to walk down two flights. Then we had to cross West Executive Avenue, which separates the Executive Office Building from the White House itself. Neither of us had rubbers, Miss Quill was wearing thin shoes, and we had to wallow ankle deep in snow, but we made it.

The mess was a gay scene. We were all stormbound together, and instinctively we set out to ignore the fact that we were about to separate for all time and to cover up our deep emotions by pretending that this was just another evening.

At the table next to ours sat Colonel Bill Draper of the air force, who served as pilot for the President's plane, and when I inquired whether he would do me one last favor, and he replied that he would be glad to, I asked him whether by any chance he knew of a helicopter that would be going out toward the Shoreham Hotel. Unfortunately, I found him singularly uncooperative. Failing there, I next tried the navy, and asked Captain Pete Aurand whether he happened to have a heavy cruiser going out Connecticut Avenue. He let me down, too, so I asked them both whether they could put me in touch with the officer who had charge of the dog teams at the Pentagon. Baffled at every turn, I finally gave up and attacked my steak.

But after dinner, when Miss Quill and I had completely abandoned hope, the break came most unexpectedly. We were just leaving the White House to go back to our offices in the Executive Office Building when the blessed officer at the garage called to say that he could let us have a car at nine o'clock.

He was as good as his word, and precisely at nine we moved slowly out into the traffic. At the start we were lulled into a false sense of relief, for we moved along fairly well up past Lafayette Park, but back of the Mayflower Hotel we bogged down, stuck tighter than a cork in a bottle. Not a wheel was moving in either direction.

It was not only the snow, though that was very bad. Nor was it just the fact that the storm had hit precisely as the government offices were closing, thus trapping the great mass of commuter automobiles at the peak of the daily traffic. There was the further unique situation that while for those of us who were leaving the old administration this was the end, for those who made up the incoming group this was the beginning. We were in the midst of Inauguration Eve, and thousands of out-of-town cars were caught in the chaos which would not ordinarily have been there. Finally into all of that motionless mass there were dumped innumerable vehicles of all sorts, including chartered buses, which were trying to make their way to the big party at which Frank Sinatra was to perform.

In every lane of traffic there were abandoned automobiles. Some were out of gasoline. For others, the batteries had gone dead from long periods of standing still with windshield wipers running and lights on, and their owners had just walked off and left them where they were.

All the while the radio-telephone in our government car was crackling out messages to drivers from the dispatcher at the White House garage. Because I was an old hand I could read the code, and I was startled to learn that the First Lady had been stalled in traffic as we had been, and then infinitely relieved to learn that she had been extricated from the emergency and returned safely to the White House.

All things end at last, however, and eventually, with the combination of patience on our part and great skill on that of Sergeant Lee, who was one of the most resourceful drivers I have ever seen, we reached the Shoreham Hotel. A half hour or so later Miss Quill telephoned to say that the sergeant had also delivered her to her home, which fortunately was not far away.

Next morning we learned that some fifteen or twenty members of the White House staff never did get away, but had to stay there all night and make do as best they could. One lady from our group who had left our offices at five did not reach her home until long after midnight, and next day Admiral Arthur Radford told me that he had left Bethesda at four in the afternoon bound for the Mayflower Hotel but had not arrived until one in the morning.

It was thus that I wrote finis to the most rewarding experience of my life.